Answers from the Heart

PARALLAX PRESS · BERKELEY, CALIFORNIA

Answers
from the
Heart

PRACTICAL RESPONSES TO LIFE'S BURNING QUESTIONS

THICH NHAT HANH

PARALLAX PRESS
P.O. Box 7355
Berkeley, California 94707

Parallax Press is the publishing division of
Plum Village Community of Engaged Buddhism, Inc.
Copyright © 2009 Plum Village Community of Engaged Buddhism, Inc.
All rights reserved.
Printed in Canada.

Cover and text design by Jess Morphew.

Parallax Press would like to thank Tai Moses for her assistance.

Library of Congress Cataloging-in-Publication Data

Nhat Hanh, Thich.
Answers from the heart : practical responses to life's burning questions / Thich
Nhat Hanh.
        p. cm.
ISBN 978-1-888375-82-4
1. Religious life--Buddhism. 2. Village des pruniers (Buddhist community) I. Title.
BQ9800.T5392N45423 2009
294.3'444--dc22

                            2008050033

MR

Contents

Introduction

When you first encounter mindfulness practice, you may have a million questions. But before you look to someone else for answers, sit with these questions yourself. You may discover, with surprise, that through looking deeply and touching deeply, you can answer most of the questions by yourself.

We have the habit of always looking outside of ourselves, thinking we can get wisdom and compassion from another person or the Buddha or his teachings (Dharma) or our community (Sangha). But you are the Buddha, you are the Dharma, you are the Sangha.

The goal of this book is not to teach you about Buddhism. Storing up knowledge about Buddhism will not answer your burning questions. We have to learn the things that can help us to transform our own suffering, our own caught situations. If our teacher is a real teacher, then his or her words are there to help us be in touch with life and to untie the preconceptions, views, anger, and habit energies we have. The aim of a real teacher is to help his or her students transform.

Don't underestimate the power of a good question. A good question can benefit many people. We should ask a question from our heart, a question that has to do with our happiness, suffering, transformation, and practice. A good question does not need to be very long.

There was a famous Zen teacher in ninth century China, Master Linji. He was well-known for his "Zen Battles" between teacher and student. A student would stand up to ask a question of the master, to find out if his own understanding was ripe. Linji used the expression "coming out onto the battlefield"; sometimes the student was victorious and sometimes he was defeated. When people asked me the questions in this book, they didn't have to come out onto the battlefield. In battle there is someone who wins and someone who loses. Instead, I try to look at each question and questioner with compassion, as if I had asked the questions myself.

This doesn't mean that the answers will be what

we are wanting to hear. Just as we have the tendency to run away from a shot or a dose of medicine, even if it's good for us, we have the tendency to run away from answers that touch painful areas in our lives.

Sometimes Zen answers are like riddles, designed to stop the thinking process of the student. Thinking is not awakened understanding. Awakened understanding is quicker than lightning. Where there is reasoning, there is failure.

Sometimes the teacher has to respond by what Master Linji called "removing the object." This means that when someone comes with a question, if the teacher were to spend a lot of time explaining this and that, it wouldn't help; the student might stay caught in thinking and views. Instead the teacher removes the question, which may very well be a false obstacle. I often remove the object in order to give the question back to the student.

I hope that in some of these questions and answers we can find the kind of healing that we deeply need. The teaching words of the Buddha are called "the all-embracing sound." This means that the words have the nature of fullness, touching all kinds of human conditions. All-embracing sound also means that a teaching has the characteristic of being appropriate to the hearer; it can touch our real situation. Questions and answers are an opportunity to cultivate our capacity to listen with openness, receptivity, and stillness. Listening in this way, we will surely receive the medicine we need.

Chapter 1

Daily Life

Q. I don't know what to do with my life. I'm pulled in many different directions, but I can never stick to any one thing. I'm always unhappy and confused. What can help?

A. Sometimes we plant roses by using cuttings. Knowing that the branch has no roots, we put the cutting in moist soil. If we leave the branch for long enough in rich, damp soil, it will become stable and take root. You have the potential to become a beautiful rose bush, but you need some soil, and you need to stay in the soil long enough for your roots to grow strong.

We're used to seeing suffering as something negative. Let us learn to look at suffering as something positive. In the teaching of the Buddha, suffering is called a noble truth, and we can learn a lot from it. A human being should have the capacity to deal with both suffering and happiness. The two always go hand in hand; if there's no suffering, there's no happiness. We all have a natural tendency to avoid suffering, and that's not good for us. Without suffering we can't grow as human beings, we can't learn to become more understanding and compassionate. That's why we have to learn to recognize suffering and embrace it. So long as you continue to try to run away from it, you'll continue to suffer. Many people find themselves in the situation of being rootless. You need the proper environment, the right kind of soil, in which to take root. A Sangha, a loving community of brothers and sisters, will give you the right kind of support and you'll be on your own very soon. It doesn't take long for a cutting to become a rose bush.

Q. I feel guilty when I'm not occupied. Is it okay to do nothing?

A. In our society, we're inclined to see doing nothing as something negative, even evil. But when we lose ourselves in activities, we diminish our quality of being. We do ourselves a disservice. It's important to preserve ourselves, to maintain our freshness and good humor, our joy and compassion. In Buddhism we cultivate "aimlessness" and in fact in Buddhist tradition the ideal person, an *arhat* or a bodhisattva, is a businessless person—someone with nowhere to go and nothing to do.* People should learn how to just be there, doing nothing. Try to spend a day doing nothing; we call that a "lazy day." Although for many of us who are used to running around from this to that, a lazy day is actually very hard work! It's not so easy to just be. If you can be happy, relaxed, and smiling when you're not doing something, you're quite strong. Doing nothing brings about quality of being, which is very important. So doing nothing is actually something. Please write that down and display it in your home: *Doing nothing is something.*

Q. My desire for achievement has led to much suffering. No matter what I do, it never feels like it's enough. How can I make peace with myself?

A. The quality of your action depends on the quality of your being. Suppose you're eager to offer happiness, to make someone happy. That's a good thing to do. But if you're not happy, then you can't do that. In order to make another person happy, you have to be happy yourself. So there's a link between doing and being. If you don't succeed in being, you can't

---

* Thich Nhat Hanh, *Nothing to Do, Nowhere to Go: Waking Up to Who You Are: Reflections on the Teachings of Master Linji* (Berkeley, CA: Parallax Press, 2007).

succeed in doing. If you don't feel that you're on the right path, happiness isn't possible. This is true for everyone; if you don't know where you're going, you suffer. It's very important to realize your path and see your true way.

Happiness means feeling you are on the right path every moment. You don't need to arrive at the end of the path in order to be happy. The right path refers to the very concrete ways you live your life in every moment. In Buddhism, we speak of the Noble Eightfold Path: Right View, Right Thought, Right Speech, Right Action, Right Livelihood, Right Effort, Right Mindfulness, and Right Concentration. It's possible for us to live the Noble Eightfold Path every moment of our daily lives. That not only makes us happy, it makes people around us happy. If you practice the path, you become very pleasant, very fresh, and very compassionate.

Look at the tree in the front yard. The tree doesn't seem to be doing anything. It stands there, vigorous, fresh, and beautiful, and everyone profits from it. That's the miracle of being. If a tree were less than a tree, all of us would be in trouble. But if a tree is just a real tree, then there's hope and joy. That's why if you can be yourself, that is already action. Action is based on non-action; action is being.

There are people who do a lot, but who also cause a lot of trouble. The more they try to help, the more trouble they create even if they have the best intentions. They're not peaceful, they're not happy. It's better not to try so hard but just to "be." Then peace and compassion are possible in every moment. On that foundation, everything you say or do can only be helpful. If you can make someone suffer less, if you can make them smile, you'll feel rewarded and you'll receive a lot of happiness. To feel that you're helpful, that you're useful to society: that is happiness. When you have a path and you enjoy every step on your path, you are already someone; you don't need to become someone else.

In Buddhism, we have the practice of *apranihita*, aimlessness. If you put an aim in front of you, you'll be running all your life, and happiness will never be possible. Happiness is possible only when you stop running and cherish the present moment and who you are. You don't need to be someone else; you're already a wonder of life.

Q. Whenever I'm doing one thing, my mind wanders ahead to the next thing or back to the last thing. What can I do to stop always thinking about the path not taken?

A. When you receive several letters, you have to decide which one to read first. Perhaps there are two letters you want to read that seem equally important. Still, you have to make a decision; you have to choose one to pick up first. After making the decision, stick with it. When you're crossing a bridge, don't think of the bridge you're not crossing; you'll have to cross it eventually, but only after you cross this one first. This is our practice. The lawyer thinks only of the client he is with, not the client who is coming later. The doctor thinks only of the patient in front of him. This is concentration, mindfulness, one-pointed mind. If you haven't trained your capacity of bringing all your attention to just one object, there will be dispersion and disturbance. You have to be one hundred percent in the here and now.

Q. How can we incorporate the practice of mindfulness and living in the present moment with making plans for our lives?

A. The practice of mindfulness doesn't forbid us to plan for the future. It's best not to lose ourselves in uncertainty and fear over the future, but if we're truly established in the present moment, we can bring the future to the here and the now, and make plans. We're not losing the present moment when we think about the future. In fact, the present moment contains both past and future. The only material that the future is made of is the present. If you know how to handle the present in the best way you can, that's all you can do for the future. Handling the present moment with all your attention, all your intelligence, is already building a future.

Q. How can we become aware of and change bad habits?

A. Negative habit energy always tries to emerge, but if you are mindful, you recognize it. Mindfulness helps us to recognize the habits transmitted by our ancestors and parents or learned during our childhood. Often, just recognizing them will make them lose their hold on you. Suppose you have the habit of getting into a hurried state while doing such things as shopping or cooking. With mindfulness you recognize that you are rushing around and knocking things over, trying to finish quickly. Then you realize that the energy of being in a hurry has manifested itself. So you breathe in and out mindfully, and you say, "My dear habit energy, here you are again." And as soon as you recognize it, it will lose its strength.

If it comes back again, you do it again, and it will continue to lose its strength. You don't have to fight it, just recognize and smile at it. Every time you recognize it, it becomes a little bit weaker until, eventually, it can't control you anymore.

Q. How can I get over being so judgmental?

A. When we look at a human being, we look deeply enough to see that an individual is made of many elements: society, education, parents, ancestors, culture, and so on. If we don't see all these elements, we don't fully see the person. If he has the tendency to behave in a negative manner, it doesn't mean that he likes to behave that way, but that he may be a victim of transmission. The negative seeds in him may have been transmitted to him by his society, his parents, his ancestors, or his culture.

When you realize this, it will be easier to have compassion for him. Then you will be motivated less by the desire to judge than by the desire to do something in order to change the environment, the culture so that the next generation will not be a victim of transmission. Instead of annoyance, you can have the desire to act with compassion.

When you look deeply at yourself, and you notice

one of your strengths, whether it is talent or skill-fulness or happiness, you know you have inherited it from your ancestors, your parents, your culture, and so on. You are their continuation, they have passed these things on to you. Likewise you see the negative things in yourself, such things as fear, anger, and discrimination that may have been transmitted to you by your parents and ancestors. In either case, there is no judgment on your part. Your parents and ancestors were not able to transform themselves, that is why they have passed these things on to you. But you have an opportunity to transform so that you will not transmit these negative things to your children. This way of looking at yourself and others will give you understanding, compassion, and a desire to act in order to transform.

Q. How can we best share our joy with others?

A. When there is true joy within us, that joy will not only benefit us, but also the people around us. True joy can help our bodies and our consciousness. Joy is something that nourishes us. In Buddhist circles, the practice of meditation is described as daily nourishment. In the practice of meditation, joy and concentration are important elements. If during the

21

practice of walking and sitting meditation we don't feel joy, something is wrong with our practice.

Our joy is shared naturally because when we are joyful, we are happy and inspire others. We make the atmosphere light and the air easy to breathe, and we collaborate with others in order to create the kind of collective joy that will benefit many people. In our daily chanting we say: "I vow to offer joy to one person in the morning, and to relieve the suffering of one person in the afternoon." But that is just the minimum, because when we offer joy to one person, we are already offering joy to many people.

As your understanding grows, your compassion and loving kindness will grow, and your heart will grow larger. When our hearts are larger, we have a better capacity to receive and embrace the negative feelings we have in order to transform them. Suppose you pour a handful of salt into a cup of water; now you can't drink the water because it's too salty. But if you pour a handful of salt into a river, the river is so large it's not affected and all of us can continue to drink the water. The river is enormous, that's why it has the capacity to receive, embrace, and transform. Our hearts are like the river. They are large enough to transform suffering and bring joy, not just to ourselves but to all those around us.

Q. I tend to idealize other people, and I get disappointed when they don't live up to my expectations. What can I do?

A. One day, when I was doing the Ten Mindful Movements in front of a tree, I realized that the tree had a lot to offer me and I had a lot to offer the tree.[*] The tree gives me beauty, shade, and oxygen. I offer the tree my breath, my appreciation, and my joy. The tree and I are interconnected. When we look at a human being, we can look in exactly the same way, without exaggerating what is there or imagining what is not there. Sometimes we expect too much, we want to idealize what we see. If when we see something or someone, we can acknowledge reality as it is without exaggerating or imagining, we will suffer less. Many people love the Buddha, but they distort the Buddha, they make the Buddha into a god, a creator. When they do this it harms them and it harms the Buddha. That's why the practice of mindfulness, the mere recognition of things as they are, is the basic practice of Buddhism. "Breathing in, I know this is my in-breath. Breathing out, I know this is my

---

[*] The Mindful Movements are contemplative exercises designed to cultivate awareness of the body and breath. See the DVD and book *Mindful Movements* by Thich Nhat Hanh and Wietske Vriezen (Berkeley, CA: Parallax Press, 2008).

out-breath." "Breathing in, I see the blue sky. Breathing out, I smile to the blue sky." Recognizing things as they are will prevent you from exaggeration and imagination.

Q. I have a lot of trouble letting go of things: relationships, jobs, feelings, and so on. How can I reduce these attachments?

A. To "let go" means to let go of *something*. That something may be an object of our mind, something we've created, like an idea, feeling, desire, or belief. Getting stuck on that idea could bring a lot of unhappiness and anxiety. We'd like to let it go, but how? It's not enough just to want to let it go; we have to recognize it first as being something real. We have to look deeply into its nature and where it has come from, because ideas are born from feelings, emotions, and past experiences, from things we've seen and heard. With the energy of mindfulness and concentration we can look deeply and discover the roots of the idea, the feeling, the emotion, the desire. Mindfulness and concentration bring about insight, and insight can help us release the object in our mind.

Say you have a notion of happiness, an idea about

what will make you happy. That idea has its roots in you and your environment. The idea tells you what conditions you need in order to be happy. You've entertained the idea for ten or twenty years, and now you realize that your idea of happiness is making you suffer. There may be an element of delusion, anger, or craving in it. These elements are the substance of suffering. On the other hand, you know that you have other kinds of experiences: moments of joy, release, or true love. You recognize these as moments of real happiness. When you have had a moment of real happiness, it becomes easier to release the objects of your craving, because you are developing the insight that these objects will not make you happy.

Many people have the desire to let go, but they're not able to do so because they don't yet have enough insight; they haven't seen other alternatives, other doorways to peace and happiness. Fear is an element that prevents us from letting go. We're fearful that if we let go we'll have nothing else to cling to. Letting go is a practice; it's an art. One day, when you're strong enough and determined enough, you'll let go of the afflictions that make you suffer.

Q. Can mindfulness practice help us live with our sexual energy and remain loyal to our spouses and partners?

A. Sexual energy is normal; we should not look upon it as something evil. We all have our animal nature. The practice of Buddhist meditation, the practice of service, of compassion, is not something that opposes our animal nature. The Buddha nature in us can very well embrace the animal nature in us. There's no need for a fight between the two; such a struggle would be destructive and cause a lot of damage within us. Buddhist practice is based on the insight of nonduality. We are mindfulness, but we are also forgetfulness. We are compassion, but sometimes we are anger and hatred. And all of them form a community within us. We don't have to exclude or suppress anything, including our sexual energy.

Mindfulness is the capacity to recognize what is there without being attached to it or fighting and suppressing it. That is called simple recognition. The first step in mindfulness is simply to recognize and embrace what is there whether it is positive or negative, pleasant or unpleasant. Then, if our mindfulness is strong enough, we can know the nature of what is there and how to transform the energy and channel it in a good direction. Sexual energy is only one kind of energy; it can be channeled in other directions. If you're interested in doing and realizing other things, then your sexual energy can be channeled in those directions and you won't have a lot of time to think about sex.

Monks and nuns recognize that sexual energy is there, but with the support of the Sangha we learn to invest our energy in other directions, toward our highest aspirations. We devote time to studying and learning the Dharma, and we discuss how to put it into practice. We are each responsible for the well-being and practice of another monk or nun, our "second body." We devote time to taking care of our second body. We also devote time to helping those who come to us to practice. We can be very happy devoting our energy in these directions. If you organize your life intelligently and direct all of your energy skillfully, and if you're capable of helping other people suffer less, then sexual energy will no longer be a major problem in your life.

In Buddhism, the teaching of love is crucial. Loving kindness, compassion, joy, and equanimity are the elements of true love, and we can practice them every day. But love is different from sexual pleasure. If the sexual act takes place without deep love, commitment, and mutual understanding, it can bring a lot of suffering and destruction. With deep understanding and communication, happiness becomes possible. With mindfulness and the practice of understanding and compassion, sexual life can be beautiful and holy.

Q: Are nudity and sexuality in art, photography, and film to be avoided? Or can sensuality be approached with mindfulness?

A: The human body is beautiful and sexuality can be something beautiful and spiritual. Without sexuality, a Buddha cannot come into the world. We can't separate mind from body; our bodies are as sacred as our minds. That's why when we look at the body as an item of consumption, an object of desire, we haven't truly seen the body. Our body should be treated with utmost respect. When we touch someone else's body, we touch their mind and their soul.

The Buddha taught that the human being is made of five elements: body, feelings, perceptions, mental formations, and consciousness. These five elements rely on each other in order to manifest. Consciousness is not something that can manifest without the body. That is why the insight that body and spirit are one is very important. When you respect someone, you respect her body, not only her feelings, perceptions, and consciousness.

Sexuality can appear in works of art. But if you show the human body in a way that only waters the seed of craving, then you are sowing seeds of future suffering in yourself and others. There are poets, photographers, and filmmakers who are capable of presenting the human body as an object of contemplation and veneration. When the human body is shown in that way, the seeds of beauty, joy, respect, and veneration that are there in the viewers can be watered. This is how it must be done. We have to show the body in such a way that inspires confidence, happiness, and joy.

Q. I can't imagine living without my camera or my cell phone. Is it wrong to be attached to these conveniences?

A. It's wonderful to have a camera—and it's wonderful not to have a camera. Mindfulness helps us to see the pleasure in owning a camera without exaggerating that pleasure. Mindfulness helps us to be at peace when we don't own a camera. I think we have the tendency to want to see things as lasting for a long time, we want to keep things with us, and we also want to share with people we love the things we have lived and seen. These are all justifiable reasons for having a camera, but when we see a newer, more expensive camera and want to throw ours away and upgrade to this better camera, that is not good. Because of that weakness in us to want to consume, manufacturers continue to produce more and more goods, and we pollute the world with the castoffs. And in order to consume a lot, we have to be very busy working all the time, leaving no time to love, to build up brotherhood and sisterhood. We have to practice a simpler style of living so we don't feel the need to consume too much. A simple life can bring a lot of happiness.

Q. What is the Buddhist view of multiculturalism? Is it possible to identify as a person of color, while at the same time not be too attached to it?

A. Each of us has elements of many other cultures and colors in ourselves. We're not "pure." So although it is fine to identify with one particular color, it's more useful I think to speak in terms of cultural and spiritual values. These are universal; everyone can appreciate and agree on them. If we believe that wherever we go, our ancestors go with us, then we can set up an ancestral altar so we are always with our ancestors. This helps us maintain our confidence in our own cultural heritage. When we have confidence in the beauty of our culture, we are capable of maintaining it, even if others don't understand it. If we don't take the time to tell our children about our culture, they'll lose it. But we also have to be aware that in each culture there are flowers and garbage, and there is no need to idealize one culture or denigrate another. If we are so attached to our particular heritage that we hold on to every aspect of it, even those that are no longer useful to us, then we are only hurting ourselves. Connecting to our ancestors and seeing them fully is a way to appreciate and identify with our particular heritage without being blinded by attachment to it.

Q. How can we practice consistent mindfulness in a world that seems to demand hurrying and rushing wherever we go? Is it possible to be mindfully busy and mindfully hurried?

A. Beginners find mindfulness easier when they do it slowly. But if your mindfulness is more advanced, you can do things more quickly. Just make sure you are being mindful. You can walk mindfully, but you can also run mindfully. It's a matter of planning. It should become a habit to plan in such a way that we have plenty of time to do each thing and we don't have to rush. Suppose you have to be at the airport at ten o'clock. Try to plan so that you have plenty of time; if possible add another hour in order to have the pleasure of doing walking meditation at the airport. When you drive, instead of thinking of your destination, enjoy every moment of the drive. When you make your breakfast, transform breakfast preparation into a meditation session, a practice of mindfulness. Try not to think of what you're going to do after breakfast. Enjoy every moment and you'll bring joy to the whole family. The secret is to dwell in the here and the now and to be happy in that moment.

Of course, we all have a lot to do; even monks and nuns have a lot of things to do. But we have learned to do them with joy, and not to consider the things we do as hard labor. That is an art to be cultivated, and every one of us can do it. If we know how to consume less, we don't have to work as hard, we don't need a bigger salary and a more expensive car to be happy. If we know the art of simple living, then we have much more time to live our lives happily and to help other people.

Q. I've been trying to practice loving speech and listening at work, but my colleagues respond with a lot of cynicism.

A. Patience is part of compassion. When we're truly compassionate, we have the capacity to wait and to be patient. People respond with cynicism and suspicion because they've met with negative situations in the past. They don't trust easily. They haven't received enough understanding and love. They suspect that what we offer them is not authentic love and compassion. Even if we really do have love and understanding to offer, they're still suspicious.

There are many young people who haven't received understanding and love from their family, parents, teachers, or society. They don't see anything beautiful, true, and good. They wander around seeking something to believe in. They're like hungry ghosts. In the Buddhist tradition, we describe hungry ghosts as having a big belly and a very tiny throat, as slender as a needle. They're famished, but their ability to swallow food is very limited. Hungry ghosts are hungry for love and understanding, but their capacity to receive it is very small. You have to help bring the size of their throat back to normal before they can swallow the food that you offer. That requires the practice of patience, continued loving kindness, and understanding. It takes time to win their trust. Until then, you can't help them. Even when faced with cynicism or suspicion, you have to continue with your practice; you have to be patient.

Q. What is the one thing that ordinary people can do every day that will bring them closer to happiness?

A. Walking meditation is the one thing that everyone can do. There are those of us who find it difficult to practice sitting meditation, but almost everyone walks. And if you are in a wheelchair you can do rolling meditation. Everyone, whether they are in Berkeley, New York, Amsterdam, Paris, or Bangkok, can enjoy mindful walking; and every time they make a mindful step, they stop their forgetfulness, they go back to life, touching the wonders of life for their healing and transformation. Walking meditation is very pleasant, transforming, and healing. When you practice walking meditation, you include your body and your mind. You also include your breath; following your breath, body and mind come together. You become fully present, fully alive, and you get closer to the happiness you're seeking.

Chapter 2

Family, Parenting, and Relationships

Q. How can we ensure that our home lives remain peaceful even when the world outside is not?

A. In every home there should be a room, you can call it the breathing room or the meditation room or the island of peace. Many of us do not have extra space or an additional room that we can use just for this. In that case, even a small corner of a room can function as a peaceful island. Any time members of the family don't feel safe or stable or strong, they can take refuge in that island of peace. It doesn't need to be very big and it doesn't need a lot of furniture; just a few cushions, a bell, and a flower. The flower represents freshness and beauty and hope.

Every time you're disturbed by your anger or frustration, even if you're a child, you have the right to take refuge in that room. Any civilized home should have such a room. That is a territory of peace, a place to take refuge in the island of self. The moment this "island" is established, you, and others too, begin to profit from it. When you step into that room, you feel a territory of peace within.

If parents are quarreling and causing their child a lot of suffering, the child may like to leave that place and go to the breathing corner or room. She can enter, invite the bell, and practice mindful breathing. She can take refuge in the peace that is there. And if the child is practicing like that, the parents may stop quarreling with each other when they hear the bell and feel the need of the child not to suffer. So the practice of one person can help the rest of the family.

When one partner is angry with the other, she can go to that room and practice mindful breathing and listening to the bell to calm herself. That practice will inspire the child and inspire the couple also. Before starting the day, the whole family might spend a few minutes in the breathing room looking at each other mindfully and happily and wishing each other a happy day. You will have started your day well by calming yourself, looking at each other, and recognizing each other as precious. Before going to sleep, you can spend a few minutes listening to the bell and breathing in and out together as a family. And every time the family has the need to listen to each other, you can use the place to practice sitting mindfully and listening deeply to the suffering of the family. When the child takes refuge in that territory, the father has no right to pursue him and call after him anymore. You have something like diplomatic immunity when you go into that territory; no one can scold you or ask you questions anymore.

Q. How can we raise our children to be more mindful and compassionate?

A. If parents practice mindfulness and compassion in their daily lives, the children will naturally learn from them. We can't tell a child to do something if we don't do it ourselves. When I walk mindfully and breathe mindfully, my disciples follow me, walking mindfully and breathing mindfully. Sometimes I must remind them gently, but it's natural that when they see an elder practicing, they follow the practice. From time to time parents might discuss mindfulness and compassion with their children, and express their wish that their children will continue living in mindfulness and with more compassion.

When you use loving speech, you can water the good seeds in your children and inspire them to do as you have done. You don't have to punish or blame them. With right speech and by following your own practice, your children will see, and they will follow you.

Q. My adolescent daughter is anxious and easily upset. What can I do to calm her troubled emotions?

A. Many young people can't handle their emotions. They suffer a great deal. What parents can do is to teach their children that emotions are like a storm; they come, they stay for a while, and then they move on. If we know how to be our best during these moments, we can weather the storms more easily.

The practice of deep breathing, breathing with the belly, can help them deal with strong emotions. It's quite possible to teach your child to do this. When you see her in crisis, you sit down with her and say, "Darling, take my hand; let's practice breathing in and out: Breathing in, your stomach is rising. Do you see your stomach rising? Breathing out, your stomach is falling. Let's do it again: In, out, rising, falling." In a few minutes she will feel much better because you have brought your mindfulness and your stability to support her. Later on she will be able to do this by herself. The practice isn't difficult. Young children and teenagers can learn it.

We shouldn't wait for strong storms to arrive in order to start the practice. This practice should be initiated right away. If you continue to practice together for two or three weeks, every day for five or ten minutes, the practice of deep, non-thinking belly breathing will become a habit. And after that, when the emotion is about to come up, the child will know what to do. She will see that she can easily survive her emotions.

Q. My teenage son and I argue all the time. How can I stop these fights?

A. The first thing you can do is to look at yourself, to see whether you have enough calm energy to help calm him when he is in your presence. The problem may not only be with the child, but within the parent. If the parent is not peaceful, this can trigger negative emotions in the child, especially if there are negative seeds planted in him. In the past there may have been times when you got irritated and reacted in a state of annoyance—this has deposited those seeds in him. You have to undo this in the present moment. Being loving and calm and having the capacity to listen can absorb a lot of suffering. If you can engage him to talk to you about his difficulties by practicing deep, compassionate listening, that will help remove the kinds of energies that are making him suffer. If you have loving kindness and the energy of peace in you, even without speaking you can influence another person and he or she will feel better just sitting with you.

Q. Some people say that mothers who work outside of the home don't take good care of their children. But what if a woman stays home and still doesn't pay much attention to her children? How can we parent while still doing the other things in our life that require attention?

A. There should not be any oversimplification of the problem; we can do both. If you manage to provide your child with enough affection, of course you can go and work. Affection is crucial for communication and understanding. Affection brings about love, and love brings about deeper understanding, and deeper understanding brings about more love.

Many parents need to work outside the home for financial reasons. Many also enjoy working. But staying home and taking care of the children and the home, and being a haven that's refreshing and healing for others in the family is also very important work. We shouldn't evaluate the value of our self or our work in terms of salary alone. We all have to learn how to be in such a way that can bring about solidity, confidence, faith, and joy.

If a parent who stays home is not able to bring about that quality in the environment, then staying home is not a positive thing. The parent who goes out to work and who comes home still fresh, loving, and smiling knows how to preserve her quality of being. The value of the action depends very much on the value of non-action, namely the quality of our being.

Q. I had abusive parents and I'm still very angry with them. How can I avoid passing this anger on to my own children?

A. If you're a victim of childhood abuse, practice looking deeply to see that your parents did not have a chance to encounter the Dharma or a wise teacher or to have good friends. They may have been brought up in an environment that allowed the seed of abuse to manifest. If they had lived in a better environment, they might have behaved differently. That is true of everyone. Now, since they have transmitted that negative seed to you, and you are determined to practice in order not to repeat their mistakes, not only will you not abuse your own children, but you will help other people of your generation to protect children. And with that intention, making that vow, you'll be able to heal and transform your suffering, including the suffering that's been caused by your parents' abuse.

Learning to look with the eyes of compassion is a precious, wonderful teaching. If you know how to look at other people with the eyes of compassion, you don't suffer anymore, and your way of looking at others makes them feel better. It's a wonderful thing to practice. The first verse in the book of practice for novices is, "Waking up this morning, I smile. There are twenty-four brand new hours for me to live. I vow to live them fully and learn to look at people with the eyes of compassion." You celebrate your twenty-four brand new hours and you make the vow to look at everyone with the eyes of compassion. It's a very beautiful way of living.

Compassion is born from understanding. Once you understand the situation of a person, you see that he or she is a victim of that situation. And when you realize that, you no longer condemn, judge, or accuse. Compassion can be born in your heart. That person does not need punishment. That person needs help. Once you see that, you don't suffer anymore. You're capable of doing exactly the opposite of what your parents have done to you. That's a wonderful transformation.

Q. How can those of us who had a painful childhood get past our pain and learn to trust people again?

A. Many of us have a wounded child within. When we've been deeply wounded as children, it's hard for us to trust and love, and to allow love to penetrate us. Because we are so busy, we don't have time to go back to our wounded child and be with her to help with the healing. Many of us are afraid to go back to ourselves and be with that child. The block of pain and sorrow in us is so huge and overwhelming that we run away from it. But in this practice, we are advised to go home and take care of our wounded child, even though this is difficult. We need instructions on how to do this so that we are not overwhelmed by the pain inside. We practice cultivating the energy of mindfulness to become strong enough. With this energy, we can go home and embrace our wounded child within. The practices of mindful walking, mindful sitting, and mindful breathing are crucial. Also, our friends' energy of mindfulness can help us. Maybe the first time we need one or two friends—especially those who have been successful in the practice—sitting next to us, to lend us their support, mindfulness, and energy. When a friend sits close to us and holds our hand, we combine her energy with our own and we can go home to ourselves to embrace our wounded child within.

You have to talk to your wounded child several times a day. Embracing your child tenderly, you reassure him that you will never let him down again or leave him unattended. If you have a loving Sangha, your practice will be easier. To practice alone, without the support of brothers and sisters, would be too difficult for beginners. Your wounded child may represent several generations. Maybe your parents and grandparents also had a wounded child within that they did not know how to handle, so they transmitted their wounded child to you. Our practice is to end this vicious cycle.

People suffer because they have not been touched by compassion and understanding. If we generate the energy of mindfulness, understanding, and compassion for our wounded child, we will suffer much less. Then we can allow people to love us. Before, we were suspicious of everything and everyone. Compassion helps us relate to others and restore communication.

Q. I've been caring for my elderly parents for several years. I love them, but it's a financial and physical

burden, and I'm finding it more and more difficult. What can I do?

A. Caring for our parents comes not only from a sense of responsibility and duty, but from a foundation of love. When love and gratefulness are at the foundation of our action, we don't get tired, we don't feel despair. So the essential practice is to look deeply in order to understand and to make love the foundation of our action and our care, and we will not get tired or discouraged. Serving our parents, taking care of our parents is taking care of ourselves.

There have to be moments when you and your parents sit down and talk to each other so that there can be mutual understanding and everyone will know their limits. With that understanding and compassion, your situation will become very different, much more pleasant. When you take care of your newborn baby, you don't think that your newborn baby is someone else; it's you, yourself. So even if you have to stay up late into the night, if you have to wake up several times during the night, you don't complain. Because you have love, you have the insight that you and your baby are one. If we can see and behave like that, we have a lot more energy to continue.

Q. A loving relationship should be made up of two equal partners. How can we ensure that the stronger of the two does not overpower the weaker one and swallow him or her?

A. As soon as the concept "one" appears, the concept "two" also appears. It's like right and left. Reality should transcend the concepts of one and two. If you put the teaching into practice, you will find the answer on your own. The principle of the practice is equanimity, using the wisdom of nondiscrimination.

The right hand never tells the left that it is a good-for-nothing. The right hand does not discriminate against the left nor take pride in itself, because it deeply knows that it is at one, or "non-two," with the left hand. Every time the left hand needs it, the right hand comes and takes care of it without insisting that it is the better, stronger hand. In a relationship, it's possible to have this wisdom of nondiscrimination. When we are capable of living with each other like that, there is no stronger or weaker person, no taking advantage of the other. If there is a tendency to take advantage of the other, it means that the wisdom of nondiscrimination is not yet present.

Q. I've been practicing compassionate listening but it is very difficult to listen to people who rant and rave. How long is it necessary to practice compassionate listening?

A. Many people feel the need to talk all the time. This has become a habit for them. Although their friends may have already heard what are saying, they keep repeating the same things over and over again. The true practice of deep listening is something that can help people say the things they have never been able to say. The most precious opportunity is to be heard by someone who has the capacity for deep listening; it can bring people great relief. But in this case such deep listening is not helpful, because this person is not saying anything new; he is repeating the same thing. And that same thing is watering the negative seeds in him and in us. So allowing this practice to continue doesn't help either person.

We have to say, "Dear friend, I have already heard what you are saying. There's no use in repeating the same thing over and over again. You know there are blocks of suffering within you. But you haven't had the opportunity to recognize them, to look deeply into them and find out the source that nourishes those blocks of suffering; that is why you haven't been able to transform. That is why your suffering continues to be expressed in a way that can make you suffer and make the people around you suffer. So the solution is not to talk about it, but to recognize these blocks of suffering and to find out the causes, the kinds of food that have brought them about in you. Recognizing suffering and cutting off the source of suffering is our practice. And I'd like to help you, my dear, to do so. Because I have done the same thing for myself, I've been able to free myself. I don't complain anymore, because I've been able to recognize the blocks of suffering in myself. I've embraced them and looked deeply into them. I've found their foundation, their roots, and I've practiced in order to stop nourishing them, so that I can transform. I would like to help you to see you are doing the same thing, and I will do everything in my power to help you." With loving speech, we can encourage our friends to begin the practice, to embrace their suffering, look deeply into the nature of the suffering, and begin the work of transformation and healing.

Q. My mother-in-law is very critical. I try to be tolerant of her, but sometimes I get exasperated. What will change this?

A. Your mother-in-law is the mother of your partner; that is very important. Your partner is a part of
her and her lineage. You have made a commitment
to share your partner's happiness and suffering, and
your mother-in-law is a part of that. Your mother-in-
law can be both a source of happiness and sorrow for
you and your partner. That is why your practice has
to embrace her; your partner's happiness depends
very much on your in-laws' happiness. If your partner is not happy, it will be difficult for you to be
happy. Taking care of your in-laws is taking care of
yourself and your partner.

You have to learn to take care of whatever belongs
to your partner because you care about her well-being
and happiness. That is why you have to look far and
wide and recognize everything and everyone that is
linked to her, so that you can really make her happy.

We must be polite. When you go to your in-laws'
house, you greet them politely, because they are
your wife's parents. Whether or not your mother-in-
law is loving, your behavior and capacity to respect,
embrace, and help her is related to your own and
your partner's happiness. That is why, with looking
more deeply, the boundaries will be removed and you
will be able to accept her as an important ancestor of
your partner.

Q. My father and I had a difficult relationship. We could not talk or listen to each other, and now he is dead. Is it too late for us to find reconciliation?

A. Your father is still there, alive, in every cell of your body. You are the continuation of your father. He didn't have the chance to encounter the Buddha-dharma, the art of making peace inside and outside. But he is lucky to have you to continue him, and the transformation will not only be yours, but his. He will profit from your practice.

Your father can be with you in any moment. When you practice breathing in, and you feel joy and peace, you say, "Father, do you feel the joy and the peace? We are practicing together." When you walk, you walk for your father as well. This is a practice of love. He has the Buddha nature in him, the capacity to be sweet and kind, but he did not have the chance to develop that side of himself. You are going to help him develop that aspect of his being.

You can do this through the practice of deep listening, because your father in you needs to be listened to. And the little girl in you, she is still alive and she wants to be listened to. You don't need another person in front of you in order to practice deep listening. You just sit there at the foot of a tree or on the grass, and you listen to your father inside, and to the little girl who was you. To listen to her is to listen to yourself. Listening to your father is also listening to yourself. The quality of the listening can be very high, very deep, if we know how to be really present, how to bring the mind back to the body and establish ourselves fully in the here and the now. That deep listening will bring about a lot of insight, a lot of transformation and healing. You can also write a letter to your father: a concrete, deep, honest letter. That will bring about true reconciliation within, because that letter is not only for your father, it is also for you.

Q. Being single brings me a lot of pain. I know I am fortunate to have a loving family and friends, but I still wish I had a partner to share my life with. How can I handle this ache when it comes?

A. We all share the fear that our need to love and be loved cannot be fulfilled. The fear of being lonely is always there, in everyone. We have to recognize that fear and that need within ourselves. The practice is to look deeply into that kind of fear. To love is to offer understanding and comfort. Understanding is the source of love. We would feel miserable if no one understood us. And when someone does not understand us, he or she cannot love us. Without understanding, love is impossible. So the truth is that we need understanding and we need love. And we are looking for someone who can provide us with both.

Suppose there is someone who is capable of offering us understanding and love. Suppose he is somewhere there, she is somewhere there. But we have to ask the question: Are we capable of offering him or her understanding and love? Are we capable of generating the understanding and the love that we so need? Because if we're not capable of generating the energy of understanding, nothing will happen.

The teaching of the Buddha aims at helping us to generate the energy of love and understanding. If we can produce that energy, it will first of all help us to satisfy our need to be loved. And then, with that capacity of love and understanding, we can embrace the people who are with us now. We can make them happy while we are happy ourselves. Happiness creates more nourishment, healing, and happiness.

So the question is not: How can we obtain love and understanding? The question is whether we have the capacity of generating love and understanding ourselves. If we do, we'll feel wonderful, because these energies satisfy us and the people around us at the same time. That is the love of the Buddha. True love is like that too. Loving one person is really an opportunity to learn to love all people. If you have the capacity to love and to understand, you can do that now, you don't have to wait. When we succeed in this, our worry and fear go away, and we feel wonderful right away.

Q. When a relationship ends, my feelings of sadness, anger, and jealousy last for weeks and even months. How can I turn the page on these painful feelings?

A. The break in a relationship is a collective creation. When two people don't know how to treasure their relationship, how to handle their feelings of anger and frustration, how to practice loving speech and deep listening, they may make a mess of their relationship. Feelings of fear, sorrow, regret, anger, and despair are the outcome. There is a tendency to push these feelings away, because thinking about the relationship allows those feelings to overwhelm us. That is not mindfulness. Mindfulness is the practice of mindful breathing in order to have enough energy to recognize the feelings, embrace them, be one with them, and not be overwhelmed by them. You're much more than your sorrow, anger, and despair. There's a buddha in you. You have the capacity to learn, to understand, to be compassionate. The practice is to call on these wholesome energies and to sit with our sorrow and our sadness. The pain you're experiencing now may be your opportunity to learn how to build a future. Your sorrow and anger will give you a lot of wisdom. Have the courage to look deeply, to accept these feelings and say, "Hello my pain, my sadness, I know you are there, I want to take care of you, I want to understand you, and I want to learn together with you." Even fifteen minutes of this can bring some healing. Don't be afraid. You have built your own sadness; you can begin to build your own joy.

Q. Why are our most challenging relationships with the people with whom we are closest?

A. Because we are with them twenty-four hours a day. It's very clear that if we don't have a happy, harmonious relationship with our family and our Sangha, helping others will be very difficult. The practice offered by the Buddha is very precise and very clear about how to make ourselves more pleasant, more enjoyable to be with, and how to help others to transform also. In fact, that is the basic practice. In our community of monks and nuns we practice the same way. We know that if we don't have happiness inside our community, if we don't have enough brotherhood and sisterhood to nourish us, then going out to offer retreats and meditation practice will be artificial. So, the practice of transforming ourselves and transforming our communities and our families is the foundation of everything.

Q. How can I forgive people who have hurt me, without condoning them or absolving them of responsibility for their behavior?

A. Healing takes place when we are capable of generating the energy of compassion and understanding. In the teaching of the Buddha, there is another energy that can heal—that is the vow, the desire, the determination to help. When we are victims of aggressive action, if we look around we see that there are other people who suffer like us, who have also been victims of misdeeds. Suddenly our compassion arises, and we make the vow to do something, to protect the people who are about to become victims, and to help those victims who have not seen the way to transformation. If we can find that desire, that willingness to help and heal, we become a bodhisattva, we are inhabited by that strong energy of the bodhisattva to go out and help.

If we don't do anything, others may become victims also. If you have the energy of a bodhisattva, if you want very much to do something, if you want to go out and protect children and others, that's also a very powerful energy that can heal the wound inside us. With the energy of compassion and the energy of the great vow, we can follow the path of Samantabhadra, the bodhisattva of great vows, to protect and to heal others. Our compassion can embrace our family and our society, and the healing can be absolute.

Q. Some of us have done terrible things in our past and continue to suffer guilt over how we've harmed others. Is it possible to move past this kind of pain?

A. We have to find insight. Insight is at the foundation of any kind of practice. The insight is that by practicing, not only can we take care of the present, we can also take care of and change the past and the future.

Suppose yesterday you produced a thought that's not worthy of you, a thought that doesn't go in the direction of understanding and compassion; and today you regret that you have produced such a thought. You know such a thought has had a bad effect on your body, on your physical and mental health, and on the health of the world. You regret that you produced such a thought yesterday. So dwelling in the present moment, you produce another thought, a very different kind of thought, a thought that goes in the direction of understanding and compassion. If you know how to give rise to such a thought, it will catch up with the thought of yesterday and neutralize it. That is the law of karma. You can transform the karma of the past by producing positive karma in the present moment.

I met a Vietnam War veteran who confessed that his actions had caused the death of five children in Vietnam. After the war he was not at peace. He couldn't tell anyone what he'd done. He couldn't stand to be around children. He lived with this anguish and suffering for many years. Finally, he came to a retreat, and feeling our love and trust he eventually felt safe and told us what had happened.

I said, "Okay, you have killed five children. But you are still alive. Why do you shut yourself up in that prison of regret? There are children who are dying in this very moment because no one is trying to save them. You can save one or two or three children right now. If you're able to do that, then you neutralize what was in the past. You become a new person. You may have killed five, but you can save fifty. Your life becomes the life of a bodhisattva."

With that insight the man was transformed right away. His life today is completely different. He made a vow, a commitment, to use his life, his time and energy to save children in the world. That moment when consciousness is transformed is decisive. From then on, everything will be transformed. That is why you shouldn't regret the past. There are things you can do in the present moment that can neutralize the past and assure a good future.

Q. How can we influence members of our family who aren't interested in spiritual practice or teachings, but who spend a lot of time indoors watching television and eating unhealthy food?

A. We can embody the insight and the practice. When we try to impose our ideas on others, we get a strong reaction. We shouldn't preach or blame, we should just use skillful means in order to help others to realize that bringing toxins into their bodies and minds will result in suffering. The fact that you are practicing, taking good care of your body and your mind, that you are healthy, smiling, pleasant, that is like a live Dharma talk for them. Your own transformation, your own peace and joy will be an inspiration for other people to follow. Don't say, "I practice and you don't, that is why you suffer." That will only irritate them. Your own transformation and healing is the most convincing element. Your smile will tell them directly about your practice and what they are missing.

Q. What is the best way to relieve my suffering and the suffering of my friends and family?

A. We all know that understanding and compassion can relieve suffering. This is not just a platitude; where there is understanding and compassion, there's relief and help for ourselves and others. Our practice is to keep that understanding and compassion alive. As busy as we are, when we take time to look a little bit deeper, we can always find more understanding and compassion to offer. Time is very precious; every minute, every hour counts. We don't want to throw time away. We want to make good use of the minutes and the hours we have left. When we focus our attention in the here and now and live simply, we have more time to do the things we think are important. We don't waste our energy in thinking, in worrying, in running after fame, power, and wealth.

Happiness is possible when you are capable of doing the things and being the things that you want to do and to be. When we walk for the sake of walking, when we sit for the sake of sitting, when we drink tea for the sake of drinking tea, we don't do it for something or someone else. These things can be very enjoyable. That is the practice of aimlessness. While you do that, you heal yourself and you help heal the world. Awakening means to see that truth—that you want to know how to enjoy, how to live deeply, in a very simple way. You don't want to waste your time anymore. Cherish the time that you are given.

Chapter 3

Spiritual Practice

Q. Why is practicing mindfulness so important?

A. Everyone is capable of being mindful. Everyone *is* mindful to a certain extent. The question is how to be more mindful. Many people are lost in worries about the future and regrets about the past. They are caught up in their projects and their fantasies, and their minds are not connected to their bodies. If the body is not united with the mind, we are not really alive. Mindful walking and mindful breathing help bring the mind back to the body, so we can be truly present in the here and now and become truly alive. Practicing mindfulness can be a kind of resurrection; suddenly, you become alive again. Mindfulness increases concentration and allows us to see things more deeply and stop being victims of wrong perception. We will create less suffering for ourselves and for other people. We will begin to taste the joy of living and help others to enjoy their daily lives. We cannot force people to practice mindfulness, but if we practice and become happy, we can inspire others to practice.

Q. One of the most frequently used terms in Buddhist teachings is "looking deeply." What does it mean to look deeply?

A. Looking deeply means being deeply aware of the object of our concentration. We use the energy of mindfulness to embrace the object and concentrate on it. We can use not only our eyes, but also our ears to look deeply. Deep looking and deep listening are essentially the same. We can listen to ourselves and others with our ears and it will yield better understanding and insight. All of us have eyes and ears, but without the energy of mindfulness to empower them, we cannot practice deep looking and listening.

We can look deeply even with our eyes and ears closed. Looking deeply into the nature of our in-breath, we don't need eyes or ears; when mindfulness is there in our mind consciousness, it does the work of looking deeply. Sometimes we can even use thinking. In many cases, thinking can lead us astray and we can get lost. But if we know how to handle our thoughts, thinking can help us see more deeply.

All of us have had the experience of reading something and fooling ourselves or being under the illusion that we've understood it. But upon rereading it or referring back to it, we find that we haven't really absorbed or understood it. The same thing is true of looking deeply. We may think it's easy to see that a flower is impermanent. We accept the flower's impermanence. But it's not through using your intellect that you touch the root of impermanence. You have to touch the nature of impermanence in a deep way in order to go beyond your notion of impermanence and the root of that notion. This is the core of the practice called insight meditation or deep looking (*vipashyana*). In order to do it successfully, you must cultivate your mindfulness and concentration, which are the powers that allow you to go deeply into the nature of things.

Q. What is the best way to nourish our *bodhicitta*?

A. Bodhicitta is the mind of love, the desire to bring relief and joy to other people. That desire is a tremendous source of energy and can make us more alive. When we study the Five Mindfulness Trainings, we realize that it's energizing to live in accordance with them.* They can help protect us, our family, and society; prevent suffering from taking place; and allow

---

* The Five Mindfulness Trainings can be found in Chapter 7 and are further discussed in *For a Future to Be Possible: Buddhist Ethics For Everyday Life* by Thich Nhat Hanh (Berkeley, CA: Parallax Press, 1993).

peace, joy, and happiness to be there. A deep under-standing of the Five Mindfulness Trainings can help you become an instrument of love and peace.

To me, the Five Mindfulness Trainings are the substance of a bodhisattva. A bodhisattva is a living being animated by the strong desire to help awaken other people, relieve their suffering, and bring them happiness. By receiving the Five Mindfulness Train-ings and being determined to live our lives accord-ingly, we become bodhisattvas and we live not only for ourselves, but for the well-being of others; our life serves as a source of energy for their happiness.

If you have that kind of desire, it will be reflected in your way of doing and looking at things. It will be in your smile and your walk, because you will have a lot of energy. You'll no longer be afraid of hardship and suffering, because your heart will be big enough to embrace it all. You'll no longer have the tendency to exclude. You'll only want to embrace the whole world. And every daily practice—walking, sitting, smiling, and breathing—will take you in the direc-tion of bodicitta.

Q. When we contemplate impermanence, do we include in that contemplation the phenomena of time and space?

A. When we touch the nature of impermanence, we also touch the nature of interbeing. Impermanence makes life possible. To be impermanent means to not be the same thing in two consecutive moments; there is always something coming in and something going out, input and output. Everything is interacting with every other thing, and therefore touching impermanence is also touching interbeing. Interbeing means you don't have a separate existence, you inter-are with everything else.

When we contemplate space, we know that space cannot be space by itself alone. Space has to inter-be with time and matter, with everything. When we look into the nature of space, we also touch the nature of impermanence and interbeing, and we can see everything else in space. We can see matter in space; we can see time in space. Suppose we talk about spring. What is spring? Spring sounds like time—spring is followed by summer, then fall and winter—but spring is very much involved with space, because when it is spring in North America, it is not spring in Australia. So we know that in space there is time, and in time there is space. Even what we call "the present moment" cannot be by itself alone. The present moment has to be with past moments and future moments.

When you look at the sun in the morning—where I sit in the morning I always see the sun rising from the horizon—you might think you are seeing the sun of the present moment; but scientists tell us that it is the sun of eight minutes ago. The image of the sun that you see is an image sent to you by the sun eight minutes ago. So the present moment has to do with space, not only with time. But you can still live in the present moment even if you know that this is the image of the sun eight minutes ago. The present moment has to do with the here and the now, and therefore time and space are not separate entities, and looking into the one, we see the all. The insight of interbeing helps us better understand the nature of nonself and the nature of impermanence.

Many teachers and philosophers such as Heraclitus and Confucius also spoke about impermanence. But the impermanence spoken of by the Buddha is not a philosophy. It is an instrument for your practice of looking deeply. Use the key of impermanence to unlock the door of reality—the nature of interbeing, of no self, of emptiness. That is why you should not look on impermanence as a notion, a theory, or a philosophy, but as an instrument offered by the Buddha so that we can practice looking deeply and discover the true nature of reality.

Q. I have been practicing alone for many years but I still find it difficult to be mindful. I can build up concentration for a few weeks, but my mind is easily agitated and something always comes along to distract me. What are your thoughts on this?

A. It is *because* our minds are agitated that we have to practice. All practitioners have their ups and downs. That's natural. But if you have a community of fellow practitioners, a Sangha to take refuge in, you will be supported in these moments when you feel down. The Sangha will encourage you and set you on your path.

Taking refuge in the Sangha is a critical task. Without a Sangha, we cannot continue our practice for long. If you have left your Sangha, you have to go back right away. If you have not been in touch with a Sangha, try your best to find one.

All of us can build Sanghas wherever we are. People everywhere need stability, calm, and mindfulness. The obstacle may be that we want to use Buddhist terms. There are many people who just want to sit and do nothing, become peaceful and calm, be mindful of every moment of their daily lives. If necessary you may refrain from using Buddhist terms; just embody the Dharma in your mindful living and be fresh and communicative. If you use Buddhist language in the beginning, you will turn people off and you will not be successful. Listen to people deeply, using loving speech. Then you will make friends. You can also have trees, rivers, and rocks as members of your Sangha. The air you breathe is one element of your Sangha. The path you use for walking meditation is an element of your Sangha. People don't need to kneel down and receive the Five Mindfulness Trainings in order to be members of your Sangha. The child you talk to, the neighbor you make friends with can be members of your Sangha. Everyone you meet, everyone you do business with, can be a member of your Sangha. Just having a group of people to talk to, to connect to, can be a kind of Sangha. You don't have to use the word "Sangha." If you invite people over for tea, don't say, "Let's have tea meditation." Say, "Let's have tea peacefully and be aware that we have some time to spend together, enjoying our tea and our togetherness." If you learn to use this kind of language, you'll soon be able to build a Sangha.

Q. It's very difficult for me to relax. I'm restless and I have trouble sitting still when I meditate. How can I become less agitated?

A. Many of us have a strong energy pushing us to move ahead. That's why we're offered the practices of sitting, walking, eating, and breathing. While eating, we enjoy every bite of food that we chew. If we're successful with one bite, we can be successful with the second and the third. The practice of eating helps us relax. The practice of walking also helps us relax. If you feel you can't relax, practice walking meditation, taking one step at a time. If you can take one step that brings solidity and rest, then you can take another step. If you are agitated or restless and don't know how to cope with that energy, you should recognize and name that energy as "restlessness" or "agitation." Breathing in, you say, "I know you, energy of restlessness." Use your in-breath and out-breath to recognize it and smile to it. Have faith in the practice. Begin with one bite of food, one in-breath, and one step. Whatever you are doing, scrubbing the floor or taking a step, breathe in and reclaim the liberty to become yourself. Then you will no longer be a victim of the energy of restlessness.

Q. Psychotherapists tell us we should have a healthy sense of self. Should strengthening our sense of self be part of Buddhist practice?

A. People working in the field of psychology often speak of our having a sense of self. But when there is a self, one tends to compare it to other selves. Out of that comparison come the ideas of low self-esteem, high self-esteem, inferiority, superiority, and equality. Low self-esteem is considered to be detrimental. We're told to strive for higher self-esteem. But high self-esteem can also be harmful. The complex of superiority brings unhappiness. It's not a compliment to say, "He's full of himself." The person with high self-esteem can make himself and others suffer. The desire to be equal, to be "just as good as" someone, also brings unhappiness. Only the person who is empty of self is happy; he has no jealousy, no hatred, no anger, because there is no self to compare.

According to the Buddha's teaching, the self is the foundation of sickness. There are many negative mental formations; when they manifest they make us and others suffer. And there are many positive mental formations that can improve our quality of being and increase our concentration and insight. We practice in order to strengthen these positive mental formations, rather than to strengthen our "sense of self." The practice of mindfulness will help these energies to manifest, and you will have a better quality of being, you will be more solid. Mindfulness is the energy that helps us to be truly present. When you are truly present, you are more in control of situations, you have more love, patience, understanding, and compassion. That strengthens and improves your quality of being. It can be very healing to touch your true nature of no-self. Psychotherapy can learn a lot from this teaching.

Q. How can we deepen our practice?

A. Deepening our practice means having a genuine practice, practicing not in form only. When your practice is genuine, it will bring joy, peace, and stability to yourself and to the people around you. I prefer the phrase "true practice." To me, the practice should be pleasant. True practice can bring life to us right away. As you practice mindful breathing, you become alive, you become real, not only when you sit or walk, but when you're making breakfast or performing any activity. If you know how to breathe in and out mindfully while making breakfast with a smile, you will cultivate freedom—freedom from thinking about the past or worrying about the future—aliveness, joy, and compassion. That is true practice, and its effect can be seen right away.

Q. I am busy from early in the morning until late at night. I am rarely alone. Where can I find a time and place to contemplate in silence?

A. Silence is something that comes from your heart, not from outside. Silence doesn't mean not talking and not doing things; it means that you are not disturbed inside, there is no talking inside. If you're truly silent, then no matter what situation you find yourself in you can enjoy the silence. There are moments when you think you're silent and all around is silent, but talking is going on all the time inside your head. That's not silence. The practice is how to find silence in all the activities you do.

Let us change our way of thinking and our way of looking. We have to realize that silence comes from our heart and not from the absence of talk. Sitting down to eat your lunch may be an opportunity for you to enjoy silence; though others may be speaking, it's possible for you to be very silent inside. The Buddha was surrounded by thousands of monks. Although he walked, sat, and ate among the monks and the nuns, he always dwelled in his silence. The Buddha made it very clear that to be alone, to be quiet, does not mean you have to go into the forest. You can live in the Sangha, you can be in the marketplace, yet you still enjoy the silence and the solitude.

Being alone does not mean there is no one around you. Being alone means you are established firmly in the here and the now and you become aware of what is happening in the present moment. You use your mindfulness to become aware of every feeling, every perception you have. You're aware of what's happening around you in the Sangha, but you're always with yourself, you don't lose yourself. That's the Buddha's definition of the ideal practice of solitude: not to be caught in the past or carried away by the future, but always to be here, body and mind united, aware of what is happening in the present moment. That is real solitude.

Q. How can we look deeply into our fear of death?

A. When we look deeply into our fear, we see the desire for permanence. We're afraid of change. Our anger, our fear, our despair are born from our wrong perceptions, from our notions of being and non being, coming and going, rising and falling. If we practice looking deeply, we find out that these notions cannot be applied to reality. We can touch our true nature, we can touch the ultimate dimension and this brings about non-fear. When we trust that insight of no birth and no death, joy becomes possible every moment of our lives.

Visualize a cloud floating in the sky. The cloud doesn't want to change. She is afraid of dying, of becoming nothing, and that is what makes the cloud suffer. But if the cloud practices looking deeply, she will find out that it's impossible for a cloud to die. A cloud can be transformed into rain or snow or ice, but a cloud cannot become nothing; it's impossible. When the cloud has found her nature of no death, she loses her fear. She comes to understand that to be a cloud floating in the sky is wonderful, but to be rain or snow falling on the earth is equally wonderful. So she's no longer victim of her fear, because she's practiced looking deeply and touched her nature of deathlessness. Nothing can die. You cannot reduce being into non-being. Life is a process of change. Without changing, life is impossible. Once you accept that with joy, there is no fear. That is the practice of looking deeply.

Q. I'm still afraid of losing my mother or another loved one. How can I transform this fear?

A. We can look deeply to see that our mother is not only out there, but in here. Our mothers and fathers are fully present in every cell of our bodies. We carry them into the future. We can learn to talk to the father and the mother inside. I often talk to my mother, my father, and all of the ancestors inside me. I know that I am only a continuation of them. With that kind of insight, you know that even with the disintegration of the body of your mother, your mother still continues inside you, especially in the energies she has created in terms of thought, speech, and action. In Buddhism we call that energy karma. Karma means action, the triple action of thinking, speaking, and doing.

If you look deeply you'll see already the continuation of your mother inside you and outside of you. Every thought, every speech, every action of hers now continues with or without the presence of her body. We have to see her more deeply. She's not confined to her body, and you aren't confined to your body. It's very important to see that. This is the wonder of Buddhist meditation—with the practice of looking deeply you can touch your own nature of no birth and no death. You touch the no-birth and no-death nature of your father, your mother, your child, of everything in you and around you. Only that insight can reduce and remove the fear.

Q. What is the purpose of going on Buddhist retreats? Why not just read a book on Buddhism?

A. The purpose of a retreat is not to teach you about Buddhist psychology or about a particular sutra. For that you can buy a book and read on your own. The purpose of the retreat is to help us untie the knots inside. There are two kinds of knots. One knot is our notions and ideas. Everyone has notions and ideas and we are attached to them, we are not free, so we have no chance to touch the truth in life. The second knot is our afflictions like fear, anger, discrimination, despair, and arrogance. All these things should be removed in order for us to be free. The things you do on retreat, like walking, sitting, breathing, smiling, and listening to a Dharma talk, should have the function of helping you undo these two kinds of knots.

The knots are embedded deeply in our mind, in our consciousness. They bind us and compel us to do things we don't want to do, to say things we don't want to say. When you listen to a Dharma talk at a retreat, the purpose of the talk is not to give you more notions and ideas; the purpose is to help you release notions and ideas. The talk should be like the rain that can touch the seeds of wisdom and freedom within you. That's why we have to learn how to listen. We're not listening to the words. We're listening in order to get free from all notions and concepts. When you go home, if you forget everything that was said on the retreat that's a good sign. You don't have to remember anything. You should go home free. We're used to having homework from school that requires us to remember many things—words, notions, and concepts—and we think this kind of luggage is useful for our life. But in terms of the practice, this luggage is a burden. So the purpose of the retreat is to help free you from the burden of knowledge, notions, and concepts and from the burden of afflictions, anger, and despair.

Q. What is the relationship between meditation and prayer?

A. In the spirit of Buddhism, anything you do that is accompanied by mindfulness, concentration, and insight can be considered a prayer. When you drink your tea in forgetfulness, you are not truly alive because you're not there, you're not mindful, and you're not concentrated. That moment is not a moment of practice. When you hold your cup and drink your tea in mindfulness and concentration, it's like you're performing a sacred ritual; and that is a prayer. When you walk, if you enjoy every step, if every step nourishes and transforms you, then every step is a prayer. When you sit in solidity and freedom, when you breathe in and out in mindfulness, when you touch the wonders of life, that is meditation and that is also prayer. So in the teaching, the practice, and the tradition of Buddhism, there is really no distinction between meditation and prayer. When you're mindful and concentrated, when you have insight, you get in touch with the Buddha, with the Sangha. When you really pray, you get in touch with Jesus, with the Kingdom of God, and getting in touch like that has to bring about transformation and healing. When there is mindfulness, concentration, and insight, there is no distinction between the one who prays and the one to whom we address our prayer. Our Christian and Jewish friends say, "Live each moment in the presence of God." If you live with mindfulness, concentration, and insight, you are always in the presence of God and your daily life becomes a prayer. Much happiness and peace will result from that kind of living.

Q. How can we avoid the trap of falling into a routine when we're chanting or praying, the trap of

going through the words or motions without pay-
ing attention?

A. When you chant or when you listen to chanting,
you have to involve your whole body and mind. If
you do so, you're in concentration, you're in mindfulness, and you become one with the Sangha.
You don't exist as an individual drop of water; you
become the river of the Sangha. The mind should be
always with the body. That's why mindful walking is
a practice that can be considered to be a prayer. You
pray with your feet when you walk with mindfulness, and you touch the Kingdom of God, the Pure
Land of the Buddha. You can see the effectiveness of
the prayer right away.

When you breathe in and out mindfully, that is
real breathing. Body and mind are united. It would
be a pity if we just prayed with our mouth, reciting
something while our mind wanders into the past or
into the future. This isn't praying, because you're not
mindful, you're not concentrated, you're not present, there can't be insight. You pray with your spirit
and body together, not simply by joining your palms
and chanting something. We should avoid the trap of
practicing only with the form. This trap is universal;
it can happen in Buddhism, in Christianity, in every

religion. Practicing like that is not effective.

I sometimes remind the Sangha, before our meals together, by saying, "Let us breathe in such a way that many persons become one person." Then everyone in the Sangha has a chance to practice in reality and not just in form. When we bow before the altar as part of a ceremony, we have another poem we can say: "The one who bows and the one who is bowed to are not separate; therefore, the communication between them is inexpressibly perfect." We all need reminders of various kinds, so we don't fall into that trap of practicing only in the form. We have to be skillful at finding ways to keep our practice alive.

Q. Should Christians who are attracted to Buddhist teachings become Buddhist?

A. The essence of Buddhism is mindfulness, concentration, and insight. There are Christians who are capable of being mindful, concentrated, and insightful, and they are already Buddhists; they don't need to wear the label "Buddhist." When they express the desire to take the Three Refuges and the Five Mindfulness Trainings, they know this practice also strengthens their faith in Christianity. If Christians come to a Buddhist practice center, they learn methods of practice that can help them generate mindfulness, concentration, and insight. When a Christian embraces the Buddhist practice correctly, she will never be uprooted from her Christian heritage. Practicing Buddhist meditation in that way not only helps her to be a better Christian, but also helps her to renew Christianity in such a way that the young generation of Christians will feel more comfortable. Every tradition, including Buddhism, should renew itself in the light of the new developments in the world.

We should not be trapped by appearances. There are people who call themselves Buddhist who in fact are not very Buddhist, because there is discrimination and dogmatism in them. They are less Buddhist than many Christians. There are many Christians who do not call themselves Buddhist, but they are more Buddhist than these "Buddhists." We have to learn to look in that way. There are enough Buddhists; we don't need to convert more people to Buddhism. The right attitude is not to encourage people to be uprooted from their own tradition. The right attitude is to urge them to go back to their tradition. With the Buddhist practice of mindfulness, concentration, and insight they should be able to do this.

Someone once asked me, "If the Buddha and Jesus

Christ were to meet today, what would they have to say to each other?" And my answer is, the Buddha and Jesus Christ are already meeting every day, everywhere. Because Buddhists are the continuation of the Buddha, and Christians are the continuation of Jesus, and they are meeting today everywhere. We should help make their meeting successful.

Q. What do you mean when you say to go back to our religious traditions? How can we do that and continue to study and practice Buddhism?

A. If you're a Buddhist, then you know that the Buddha is a root, but you're aware that the Buddha also had roots. So your roots didn't begin with the Buddha. To inquire about the Buddha and the ancestors of the Buddha is important. When you are a Christian, Jesus Christ is your spiritual root, but before Christianity there were other traditions. Therefore it's interesting and even exciting to inquire about our roots. Our roots can be very old, and our roots can also be new. We inherit things like democracy and freedom. The people who made democracy and freedom possible for us to enjoy are also our roots. Of course, we'll encounter negative aspects and elements, but that doesn't prevent us going back to our own source. Our roots are also the roots of many people around us. A person without roots, an uprooted person, cannot be happy. If we can go back to our root tradition and try to discover the real values that are there, the jewels contained in that tradition, we'll be able to benefit many people who have these same roots.

When I say that you have to go back to your roots, that doesn't mean you have to abandon the Buddhist practice that you now enjoy. But the Buddhist practice will help you to understand more deeply, so that your work of transformation and the renewing of your own tradition will be possible. It will help your heart to open and embrace the people who don't seem open and understanding enough when they try to transmit their tradition and values to the new generations.

It's possible for us to have several spiritual roots. To me, Buddhism, Christianity, Judaism and all religions belong to the spiritual heritage of humankind. We can profit from all of these traditions. We should not confine ourselves to just one tradition. If you love mangoes, you are free to continue to eat mangoes, but no one forbids you to eat pineapples and oranges. You don't betray your mango when you eat a pineapple. It would be narrow-minded to enjoy only mango, when there are so many different fruits in the world. Spiritual traditions are like spiritual fruits, and you have the right to enjoy them. It's possible to enjoy two traditions, to take the best of two traditions and live with them. That's what I envision for the future, that we remove the barriers between different spiritual traditions.

Q. Can you explain what you mean when you say we should renew our spiritual traditions?

A. Our spiritual tradition should be a living tradition, like a tree. It should bring forth new branches, leaves, flowers, and fruit. It should be a living reality, and not just something that we keep in a museum. That growth is produced by our practice, the practice of our teachers, and the practice of the community. If we don't practice, our tradition will only retain something that's not very alive; it will be only the appearance of a tradition, devoid of real life.

When you plant plum trees, you have to prune them every year and eliminate all the branches that suck nutrition from the tree but that don't offer flowers or fruits. You have to help every branch of the tree have a chance at receiving the sunshine. A tradition is like a fruit tree. We have to take care of it and prune it when necessary. The things that are no longer relevant are the things that should be removed. We want to preserve the best things in the tradition and interpret them in a way that helps young people to see the values and qualities of the tradition and how precious it is. We need courage, we have to accept some amount of pruning in order for the tradition to be healthy, because the tendency to be corrupted is always there in every religion, including Buddhism. By pruning and tending with love and care we help the tree to be more beautiful and healthy, and to offer more flowers and more fruit.

Q. My parents are fundamentalist Christians. They don't understand Buddhism and they say my wife and children and I are going to hell because we don't accept their God. How can I communicate with them?

A. If you look at God as someone who is capable of violence and punishment, and not capable of forgiveness and tolerance, then you have a wrong view of God; you've distorted God. Some fundamentalists believe there are enemies of God to be destroyed. They don't know that their way of seeing things is bound up with intolerance and the desire to punish.

For God, there is no enemy.

There are some fundamentalists who are capable of changing their views, if we know how to use loving speech and patience in dealing with them. Mutual understanding is the foundation of true peace. Help them to see the content and not the label. It is possible to say to them that to be a Buddhist is to try to protect life, to practice generosity, to protect the safety and integrity of adults and children, to refrain from sexual misconduct, to practice deep listening and loving speech, and to refuse to consume the many toxic items available in our society. We can describe Buddhist practice in this way. With the spirit of nondiscrimination, you can help your family get out of their narrow view. We should not condemn or attack. We should use loving speech in order to help them realize that their God is a little bit too small.

Five Catholic nuns once attended a mindfulness retreat I offered. On the last day the Mother Superior said, "Everything you have been sharing is wonderful. But why have you not spoken about God?" I looked at her and smiled and said, "Dear sister, could you point out one thing I have said during the last six days that is not about God?" And she laughed—she got it!

Q. What is the meaning of dreams? Should we act on their messages?

A. In the teaching of the Buddha most of us are living in a dream. We're not really in touch with reality. We have ideas and notions about reality, about ourselves, and about others, about all the things we perceive inside us and around us. That is a real dream. The practice of mindfulness and concentration helps us look deeply in order to have a correct perception of what is there, and what is there is our body, feelings, perceptions, and the objects of our perceptions. Living mindfully and looking deeply are the only way to really live our dream.

We have to take into account what the people around us are telling us, first of all about what we believe to be a non-dream. Then take into account what the people in our night dreams are telling us. Not only are the people in your dreams a product of your mind, a mental construction, but the people who sit in front of you, who surround you in your waking hours might also be a mental construction. If this is the case, you're not able to have a correct perception of what they really are.

Your dream is also a collective creation that uses the materials that are available in your store consciousness and the collective consciousness. The people you see in your dreams manifest from the depths of your consciousness, not from outside. But this is not your own, your private consciousness, because you are made of non-you elements. Your consciousness is made of the consciousness of society. So smile at what you see in your dreams. And look deeply, there may be a message for you. The message is not what the person in the dream tells you, the message is the whole dream. There may be some deep wishes, there may be some fear, there may be some resentment at the foundation of that dream.

It's very interesting to smile and to recognize your dreams and look deeply into them. But they're not more important than your day dreams. Because what you actually see and hear when you're awake is also to a great extent the creation of your mind. What you perceive to be reality is mostly your own creation. That is why the practice of being mindful so we can recognize the objects of our mind, and the practice of looking deeply so we can see whether our perception is a wrong perception or not, is very important. Many of us are dreaming, living as in a dream. That's why we need to be awakened from our dream. The teaching is a teaching of awakening. The word "buddha" means to wake up. Buddha is the one who is awakened, and Buddhism is the teaching on how to wake up.

Chapter 4

Engaged Buddhism

Q. What is Buddhism's connection to social justice, peace, and peacemaking?

A. In Vietnam we started a movement that we called "engaged Buddhism." We wanted Buddhism to be present in every walk of life—not just in the temple, but also in society, in our schools, our families, our workplaces, even in politics and the military. Compassion and understanding should be present everywhere.

There are many of us who are eager to work for peace, but we don't have peace within. Angrily we shout for peace. And angrily we shout at the people who, like us, are also for peace; even people and groups dedicated to peacemaking sometimes fight amongst themselves. If there is no peace in our hearts, there can be no harmony among the peace workers. And if there is no harmony, there is no hope. If we're divided, if we're in despair, we can't serve; we can't do anything. Peace must begin with ourselves: with the practice of sitting quietly, walking mindfully, taking care of our body, releasing the tension in our body and in our feelings. That is why the practice of being peace is at the foundation of the practice of doing peace. Being peace comes first. Doing peace is something that comes from that foundation.

The moment when you sit down and begin to breathe in, calming your mind and your body, peace has become a reality. That kind of breathing is like praying. When there is the element of peace in you, you can connect with other people, and you can help others to be peaceful like you. Together you become a body of peace, the Sangha body of peace. The practice can bring peace to us right away; and when you're more peaceful, more pleasant, you can be more effective in contacting other people and inviting them to join in the work of peacemaking. Since you're peaceful and you know how to look peacefully, speak peacefully, and react peacefully, you can persuade many people to join you in the work of promoting peace and reconciliation.

You can't have peace just by sitting down and negotiating or making plans. You have to learn to breathe in and out, to calm yourself, and you have to be able to help the other person to do like you. If there's no element of peace in you and in the other person, none of your activities can be described as genuine acts of peacemaking.

We have to practice peace in our corporations, our cities, and our schools. Schoolteachers have to practice peace, and teach their students how to practice peace. The president of a country or the head of a political party must practice peace, must pray for peace in his body and mind before he can be effective in asking other prime ministers and heads of state to join him in making peace. Ideally each peace conference would begin with walking meditation and sitting meditation. And someone would be there to guide the total relaxation in order to remove tension, anger, and fear in body and mind. That is bringing the spiritual dimension into our political and social life; that is engaged Buddhism.

Q. Many of us activists are dedicated to the cause of peace, but we see so little progress we get discouraged. How can we avoid burnout?

A. We have to know our limits. We have to organize our lives in such a way that we can continue to get the nourishment and healing that we need. The solution is in your community. If you work with a community that practices together, a Sangha, you receive the collective energy of support. When you begin to feel exhausted by your efforts, the other brothers and sisters in your community will help with the work so you can take the time to restore yourself and continue. You must also have the courage to say no, or you will lose yourself very soon, and that will not profit the world. Learning to say no is difficult, but it is not impossible. You have to serve in a way that you can preserve yourself. Doctors, nurses, psychotherapists, and teachers have to do the same; they have to preserve themselves in order to last longer for the benefit of other people. To preserve yourself is to preserve the opportunity to serve others. Preserving yourself and your compassion is the answer. And that can be done easily within a community of practice.

Q. Our planet is threatened by global warming, extinction of species, and pollution in our rivers and oceans. What can we as Buddhists do to help save the Earth?

A. The first time astronauts took a picture of the Earth from space, millions of us were moved to see our home, the Earth, a living blue planet in a vast black cosmos. The planet Earth, so alive, abundant, and beautiful, is a real Pure Land, a true paradise, and yet we living beings do not know how to cherish and protect her. Instead we are destroying her. That is why we need the Buddha.

The Buddha is not a god; the Buddha is someone who has awakened, someone who knows what is going on. The Buddha is us. So the practice of the Dharma is to help us and the people around us to wake up to the fact that we have a beautiful planet that needs our protection.* That's why enlightenment, awakening, is very important. Every one of us has the seed of awakening in us, and that is why we are hopeful. With collective awakening, things can move quickly. So everything we do should be aimed at bringing about collective awakening.

The practice of the Dharma cannot be individual anymore. It should be a collective practice. Teachers should practice with other teachers and students; psychotherapists should practice with their clients and other therapists. Filmmakers should make films that inspire awakening. Journalists should write articles that help people to wake up. Everyone has to do the work of promoting awakening. Awakening is the

---

* In *The World We Have: A Buddhist Approach to Peace and Ecology* (Berkeley, CA: Parallax Press, 2008), Thich Nhat Hanh shows how spiritual practice can heal and transform the planet and help stop global warming.

foundation of every kind of change.

In order for the Buddha and the Dharma to be available, we have to build a Sangha, a community that practices awakening. The Sangha is our refuge. By taking refuge in the Sangha, we take refuge in the Buddha and the Dharma, and we feel safe. When we're mindful, when we're concentrated, when we practice awakening, we are the Buddha, and our Sangha is the Buddha. This is something we must recognize. If we can touch that truth, we will no longer be victims of despair. Despair is the worst thing that can happen to us. Collective awakening is our hope and the hope of our planet; and collective awakening is possible.

Q: What can we do when a person attacks us physically? May we use force in order to protect ourselves? Can a country use force to protect itself?

A: There are many things we can do to prevent ourselves from being attacked, physically or mentally. These things are part of how we live our daily lives. We learn to live in such a way that nobody wants to attack us. When you know how to generate the energy of brotherhood, of compassion, you'll be protected by the energy of compassion and understanding. By living with understanding and compassion, you will also have a lot of friends to protect you. This is the basic practice. That is why we shouldn't wait until there's an attack in order to learn how to react.

When the Buddha was a young man he was versed in martial arts. He knew that with his skill, he would be able to respond to a physical attack. Like the Buddha we can practice qigong and nonviolent methods of protecting ourselves. We can eat and work and sleep in a way that we preserve our health and resilience. We can cultivate mindfulness, concentration, and compassion. Every time the Buddha was in danger of being attacked physically, he used his mindfulness, intelligence, and compassion to subdue the person who was about to attack him, and he didn't have to use his martial arts.

Misunderstanding brings fear and anger, and we immediately think of the gun and the army as the only solution. But there are many nonviolent ways to protect our country and ourselves. Violence is the last resort. When a country is united, when it has wise leaders who practice deep dialogue and deep listening, the country has many friends and doesn't have to use its army a lot. Instead the soldiers spend their time repairing roads, building bridges, and helping communities.

Q. How can we help our leaders become better?

A. Our leaders have good seeds in them and they also have negative seeds. They may be surrounded by people who don't know how to water their good seeds and who continue to water their seeds of fear, anger, violence, and greed. That's why we have to find ways to get in touch with our political leaders and help them. Protesting is a kind of help, but it should be done skillfully, so it is seen as an act of love and not an act of hate.

Political and business leaders have a lot of energy and the desire to fulfill their wishes. Some of these desires may be very wholesome: the desire to stop pollution, bring an end to social inequality, restore peace, transform and bring change into the world. But that doesn't mean that they don't also have the desire to be powerful, successful, and famous. So there may be several conflicting desires in our leaders. We can help them to become aware of their motivations and see how to harmonize them. The way is to help them to understand themselves.

Our leaders generally believe that they understand themselves and the world, and that all they have to do is act. But that's not true. They haven't understood themselves enough. They haven't understood the world enough. This is a reality. None of us understands ourselves perfectly, none of us understands the world enough. It's good for a practitioner to be humble enough to recognize that she has to learn more about herself and more about the suffering and the situation of the world.

We can help our leaders not to be too sure of their understanding of themselves and of the world. You should be able to listen to them and to use loving speech in order to help them to make progress on the path of self-understanding and understanding the world situation. When they act, we want them to act in the context of a Sangha and be able to make use of collective insight.

The practice of listening deeply to oneself and understanding oneself well, of listening to the world and understanding its suffering, is the same for everyone, whether they're individual practitioners, political leaders, or business leaders. There are many business leaders who want to do good things, who want to use their companies to promote more social equality and well-being. But they're encountering a lot of difficulties. Some of them have to make compromises or they may lose their position and their career. Our leaders have their own difficulties. We can't simply blame them for the world's problems. We have to understand them before we can help them.

There are many ways of approaching leaders. All of us—carpenters, machinists, journalists, writers, filmmakers, educators, parents, lawyers, nurses—can write letters, make phone calls, carry signs. We can express ourselves in such a way as to bring about awareness and help with the transformation of our collective consciousness. This is the work at the base; transforming the way we think, helping all of us to see things more deeply and clearly. Every one of us can do this in our daily life. That will contribute greatly to the awakening of the world. Our political leaders and business leaders will profit. We have to speak to them. We have to shine light on them. But before that we have to shine light on ourselves.

Q. Dr. Martin Luther King, Jr. was a leader with the ability and the knowledge to truly transform the world into a place of peace and cooperation. Will we ever have such a leader again?

A. Martin Luther King, Jr. is still here. There are among us more than one Dr. King; there is continuation. But we have to be very observant in order to be able to recognize his or her presence and offer our support and our help. Often, we feel that we need a leader outside of ourselves—a Buddha, a Gandhi, or a Martin Luther King, Jr.—to show the way. But we have the Buddha inside of us. We have Gandhi and King inside of us as well. We are interconnected. We don't need to wait for some other person to be the change we want to see in the world.

One of the ways we can help is to show the people who have a lot of money and guns that they can be truly happy. There are many people who are powerful and rich but who suffer very deeply. They believe that happiness isn't possible without money and power. That kind of thinking is at the very root of war and social injustice. If you can give those people a taste of true happiness they will be able to change their way of thinking. But you can't just change their thinking by talking. You have to do something else. You have to show that you are truly happy, even if you don't have a lot of money. According to the teaching of the Buddha, these people have the seed of enlightenment in them also. If we manage to touch that seed, they will abandon their way of thinking, and they will serve the cause of peace. In this way you yourself help the continuation of Martin Luther King, Jr. in the world.

Q. As a judge, how do I reconcile justice and compassion?

A. True justice should have compassion in it. When someone does something harmful, the destruction is done not only to the victim, but also to the perpetrator. We all know that every time we say something unskillful, something that can damage our relationship with the other person and make her suffer, we know that we have also done harm to ourselves, and created suffering for ourselves. That comes from our lack of skillfulness, our lack of mindfulness, and our lack of compassion, and we suffer as the other person suffers. Maybe not right now, but a little bit later we will suffer. The real cause of our harmful action is our ignorance, our lack of skillfulness.

If we know how to look at a so-called criminal, we will have compassion. Society has created him like that; he has been born into a situation in which social conditions, his parents, and other influences created his behavior; he's very much the victim of his situation. He was born into that life, and he has been a victim ever since. Nobody has helped him—educators, legislators, politicians, businessmen, humanitarians, no one has helped him, and that is why he is what he is. If you put him to death, you can call it justice, but I think that is less than justice, because he has not been helped at all.

We are products of our society and our environment to a very large extent. If we see that, if we see the nature of interbeing in the criminal act, we will be able to be compassionate, and the punishment that we propose in that case will be lighter. Looking deeply helps us to understand and to have compassion. With compassion, you can offer the kind of justice that contains more patience, understanding, and tolerance. Not only can we reconcile justice and compassion, but we can also demonstrate that true justice must have compassion and understanding in it.

Q. What are Buddhist views on capital punishment? Suppose someone has killed ten children. Why should he be allowed to live?

A. Ten people are dead; why do you want to kill an eleventh one? A man who has killed ten children is a sick person. Killing him won't help him and it won't help us. There are others like him in society, and looking at him deeply we know that something is wrong with our society that it can create people like that. Looking in the light of interbeing, we can see the other elements that have produced him. That is how understanding arises. That is how we see that this person needs help, not just punishment. Of course, he must be locked up for the safety of society, but that's not the only thing we can do.

Buddhist books on meditation, Buddhist magazines, and even Dharma talks have been offered in prisons, and many prisoners have begun to practice. A number of them have learned to live peacefully, even in prison. I get many letters from prisoners who have read my books. One wrote, "I see other inmates running up and down the staircases and I can see their suffering and agitation. I hope they can do as I do, walking up and down the staircase in mindfulness, following my breathing. When I do that, I feel peace within myself, and when I feel peace within myself, I can see very clearly the suffering of other inmates." That person has been able to give rise to the compassion within him.

So punishment is not our only option. Transformation and healing are possible in these difficult situations. Killing someone only reveals our own weakness. We don't know what to do any more, and we give up, we surrender. Killing someone is a cry of despair. But together we can practice looking deeply in order to find better means than approving of capital punishment.

Q. Suppose I work in an industry that produces toxic poisons or that sells a harmful product or that causes conflict between people. How do I reconcile helping others while working in such a field? Should I quit my job?

A. One day, a gentleman driving a luxurious car came to see me. He told me he was responsible for designing nuclear warheads. His conscience was very troubled about doing such disruptive and disturbing work, and he asked me whether he should quit his job. After some reflection I told him to continue his work—but mindfully. Despite the potentially destructive work he was doing, this engineer had a conscience. He was aware of what he was doing. The world needs mindful people working in such jobs. If this man were to resign, another less mindful person might take his job and the situation would get worse.

People with demanding jobs (construction workers, peace officers, emergency room doctors) and all of us can also be practitioners and Dharma teachers. The lawyer can practice looking deeply with compassion and understanding, and help her clients look deeply so that transformation and healing become possible. Of course the lawyer has to protect, argue, and speak for her client; but she can also speak her heart. She can tell her clients what she sees on the opposing side and help them to understand the other side's point of view. When a lawyer expresses herself in court, she can water the seeds of understanding and compassion in the hearts of everyone, including the judge. This is very important. That kind of practice will be observed and appreciated by many people.

A mindful politician can act from conscience and independent insight. He is capable of voting differently from his party, of voting mindfully. By showing honesty and good will, other members of his party will understand him and he will enjoy the support of the people. So it's very important to bring in the dimension of practice, the spiritual dimension, into your work. We need people like that in our world.

As we follow the path of becoming a fully enlightened person, a buddha, we are in training. The Five Mindfulness Trainings are needed because we're not fully enlightened yet. We don't need to practice the five trainings perfectly. If we know we're making steps in the right direction, that's good enough. The issue isn't to be perfect in all that we do, but to make steady progress on the path. If you're in a situation or a job that requires you to continue living in a way that goes against the spirit of the Five Mindfulness Trainings, then you should give rise to the hope that some day you can get out of that situation and have a vocation that doesn't harm humans and nature. Meanwhile there are things you can do. You can talk to your coworkers. You can educate other people. Having a good job is important. But being honest, living peacefully, and having a path to follow is more important. It's possible that a different, less stressful job might allow you to live a simpler and happier life. The important thing is not to make a compromise when you're determined to practice right livelihood and live with compassion and understanding.

Q. I have tremendous compassion for animals and I am a vegetarian. But in my work as a scientist I must test new drugs on animals to determine if they're safe for human beings. How do I resolve my turmoil over this?

A. If animals could organize a protest, they certainly would organize one around laboratory testing. But because we're in a stronger position, we're using them to discover ways to better the human condition. You're using animals for research that benefits human beings. You represent all of us and are doing it in our name. We're all responsible with you in this act. We all suffer with you in this act. And we are anxious to find a way to reduce the suffering of animals, plants, and minerals.

One thing you can do is tell people what's going on, because many of us are ignorant. We don't pay enough attention. We don't know how much animals suffer. You are the flame at the tip of the candle. You should wake us up and tell us what you're doing. Share with us the reality of the suffering of animals so that we can feel co-responsible with you. This can help you feel supported in your determination to live deeply and mindfully. And we will participate in your deep looking so you might sooner gain insight into ways of significantly reducing the suffering of animals.

Continue in your work, but continue mindfully. I trust that some insight will come to you later, and this insight will help you improve your work in such a way that the animals will benefit, too. Notice your compassion and don't become a machine. Remain a human being, and keep your compassion alive. Be mindful and help us to be mindful, too. You're doing it for all of us, and we're co-responsible for everything you're doing.

Q. During these terrible times of war and despair, what can artists do to contribute to the betterment of the world?

A. By living your life, by producing works of art, you contribute to the work of the collective awakening of our people. A bodhisattva is someone who is awake, mindful, and motivated by a desire to help others to wake up. The artist, the actor, the film-maker, the novelist may be inspired by a desire to become a bodhisattva, helping with the awakening of the people, helping them to touch the seed of joy, of peace, of happiness in themselves, helping them to remove and transform the seeds of discrimination and fear and craving. The artist can do all this. If you are motivated by that desire, you will have so much joy and energy that fame and power will not appeal to you anymore. Nothing can be compared with that kind of joy, knowing that your life on Earth is beautiful and is helpful.

One day in New York City I met a Buddhist scholar and I told her about my practice of mindfulness in the vegetable garden. I enjoy growing lettuce, tomatoes, and other vegetables and I like to spend time gardening every day. She said, "You shouldn't spend your time growing vegetables. You should spend more time writing poems. Your poems are so beautiful. Everyone can grow lettuce, but not everyone can write poems like you do." I told her, "If I don't grow lettuce, I can't write poems."

When I'm taking care of the lettuce or watering my garden I don't think of poetry or writing. I focus my mind entirely on taking care of the lettuce, watering the vegetables and so on. I enjoy every moment and I do it in a mode of "non-thinking." It's very helpful to stop the thinking. Your art is conceived in the depths of your consciousness while you're not thinking about it. The moment when you express it is only a moment of birth, the moment you deliver the baby. For me, there must be moments when you allow the child inside you to grow, so you can do your best and your masterpiece can contain insight, understanding, and compassion.

A work of art can help people understand the nature of their suffering and have insight into how to transform the negative and to develop the positive in themselves. Writing, making a film, creating a work of art can be an act of love. That act of love nourishes you and nourishes others. If you're happy, if you know how to live deeply every moment of your life, then deep understanding, joy, and compassion can come. Your art will reflect this understanding and will share it with others.

Q. How is it possible to enjoy life when so many others are suffering?

A. When you have a minute of peace and joy, yet feel that you have no right to be peaceful and joyful, that complex of guilt destroys your minute of peace and joy. And with the destruction of that minute of peace and joy, there's no more hope for you and for the world. So you have to retain that moment of peace and joy as the foundation for everything else. Hopelessness is the worst thing that can happen to us, especially when hopelessness becomes collective despair. It's very important to learn how to deal with despair, and not allow it to come and destroy everything, especially the wholesome things that are still left.

When we're able to breathe mindfully and joyfully, when we're able to make steps joyfully, happily, we're not being selfish; we're doing that for all our ancestors and for all the children in the world. There's no wisdom in practicing walking meditation and not enjoying it. If you're able to practice walking meditation peacefully, then the world has a chance. You have to look at things in that way. That is insight, the fruit of mindfulness. When you know that in every moment of your daily life you can make a contribution, you won't become a victim of despair and you'll encourage other people around you. If the pessimistic feeling comes, don't allow it to stay. Of course there is suffering everywhere in the world, there is suffering in ourselves, in our family, in our society. But if you are doing your best as a person, then there is hope that other people will do the same. Doing your best is your part, your contribution. And that is contagious; people see you and they will be inspired to try to do their best. The courage to live our daily life with compassion and awareness is our positive contribution.

Q. With all the madness and violence in the world, how can we keep ourselves from losing faith in humanity and giving up altogether?

A. There is a practice called "taking refuge." You want to feel safe, protected, calm. If you don't practice taking refuge, you lose your peace, your calm, your feeling of safety. You'll suffer and make others suffer. So when a situation is turbulent, overwhelming, full of suffering, we have to practice taking refuge in the Buddha—the Buddha in ourselves. Each of us has the seed of Buddhahood, the capacity of being calm, understanding, and compassionate. We take refuge in that island of safety within us, so we can maintain our humanness, our peace, our hope. This practice is so important. When you practice in that way, you become an island of peace and compassion, and you may inspire other people to do the same.

It's like when a boat is crossing the ocean. If the boat encounters a storm and everyone on board panics, then the boat will capsize. But if there is one person in the boat who remains calm, that person can inspire others to stay calm. Then there will be hope for the whole boatload of people. Who is that person who can stay calm in the situation of distress? In Mahayana Buddhism the answer is "you."

Q. The decision to have an abortion can be very difficult, but sometimes it is necessary. Is abortion always against the First Mindfulness Training?

A. Protecting life is a fundamental teaching of the Buddha. Abortion is the act of interrupting and causing damage to life; not only the life of the baby, but our own life, because when we have an abortion part of us also dies, and the effect of that death can continue for a long time. So we must do our best to live and plan our lives in such a way that we won't have to make this painful decision. The principle is preventive medicine. If we wait until the problem presents itself, then it's too late. That's why we should focus our attention on how to live, how to prepare conditions, how to prevent a situation from coming about in which we have to make a painful decision. This is the basic practice, not only for the individual, but for all of society.

Once the situation presents itself, the decision will be painful either way. We have to look deeply into each circumstance. We should not be dogmatic. We have to examine each case; we have to be flexible, intelligent, and compassionate. There is no one answer for every occasion. We need the insight of those around us, especially our circle of family and friends. It's not only a problem of our own comfort, but of not causing further suffering. If something is certain to create more suffering we should not go ahead and do it. If something can help stop suffering, we can do it. In the majority of cases, it would not be good to have an abortion. But in some cases, not to have one may cause even more suffering to the mother and many others.

If you're a practitioner and you've taken refuge in the Buddha, the Dharma, and the Sangha, the decision should be made based on the practice of taking refuge. You have to act according to the spirit of the

Buddha—mindfulness of what's happening now, of what will happen in the future, of what kind of suffering would happen if you were to go ahead and do it. Is there real compassion in your act or are you only calling it compassion? We need to act according to the spirit of the Dharma. This means the practice of being mindful, aware of what has happened in the past, what is happening right now, and what will happen in the future. We should also take into consideration the collective insight of the Sangha. The Sangha will look into our situation with concentration and mindfulness and may have some insight about what we should do. After having consulted the Sangha, after having followed the advice of the Sangha, you don't have to worry anymore. You have listened deeply to the Buddha, the Dharma and the Sangha, and now everyone will be co-responsible. You will not be alone. You have taken refuge in the practice in the deepest sense.

Q. What is the Buddhist view of homosexuality?

A. The spirit of Buddhism is inclusiveness. Looking deeply into the nature of a cloud, we see the cosmos. A flower is a flower, but if we look deeply into it, we see the cosmos. Everything has a place. The base—the foundation of everything—is the same. When you look at the ocean, you see different kinds of waves, many sizes and shapes, but all the waves have water as their foundation and substance. If you are born gay or lesbian, your ground of being is the same as mine. We are different, but we share the same ground of being. The Protestant theologian Paul Tillich said that God is the ground of being. You should be yourself. If God has created me as a rose, then I should accept myself as a rose. If you are a lesbian, then be a lesbian. Looking deeply into your nature, you will see yourself as you truly are. You will be able to touch the ground of your being and find peace.

If you're a victim of discrimination, then your way to emancipation is not simply by crying out against injustice. Injustice cannot be repaired by recognition alone, but by your capacity to touch the ground of your being. Discrimination, intolerance, and suppression stem from lack of knowledge and lack of understanding. If you're capable of touching the ground of your being, you can be released from the suffering that has been created in you through discrimination and oppression.

Someone who discriminates against you, because of your race or the color of your skin or your sexual orientation, is ignorant. He doesn't know his own ground of being. He doesn't realize that we all share the same ground of being; that is why he can discriminate against you.

Someone who discriminates against others and causes them to suffer is someone who is not happy within himself. Once you've touched the depth and the nature of your ground of being, you'll be equipped with the kind of understanding that can give rise to compassion and tolerance, and you will be capable of forgiving even those who discriminate against you. Don't believe that relief or justice will come through society alone. True emancipation lies in your capacity to look deeply.

When you suffer because of discrimination, there's always an urge to speak out. But even if you spend a thousand years speaking out, your suffering won't be relieved. Only through deep understanding and liberation from ignorance can can you be liberated from your suffering.

When you break through to the truth, compassion springs up like a stream of water. With that compassion, you can embrace even the people who have persecuted you. When you're motivated by the desire to help those who are victims of ignorance, only then are you free from your suffering and feelings of violation. Don't wait for things to change around you. You have to practice liberating yourself. Then you will be equipped with the power of compassion and understanding, the only kind of power that can help transform an environment full of injustice and discrimination. You have to become such a person—one who can embody tolerance, understanding, and compassion. You transform yourself into an instrument for social change and change in the collective consciousness of mankind.

Q. How can Israelis and Palestinians learn to heal their differences?

A. We are separated by labels, by words like "Israeli," "Palestinian," "Buddhist," "Jew," and "Muslim." When we hear one of these words, it evokes an image and we immediately feel alienated from the other group or person. We've set up many habitual ways of thinking which separate us from each other and we make each other suffer. So it's important to discover the human being in the other person, and to help the other person discover the human being in us. As human beings we're exactly the same. But the many layers of labels prevent other people from seeing you as a human being. Thinking of yourself as or calling yourself a "Buddhist" can be a disadvantage because if you wear the title "Buddhist" that may be an obstacle which prevents others from discovering the human being in you. The same is true whether you are Christian, Jewish, or Muslim. This can be an important part of your identity but it is not the whole of who you are. People are caught in these notions and images and they cannot recognize each other as human beings. The practice of peeling away all the labels so that the human being can be revealed is truly a practice for peace. Because people are very attached to these names and labels, it is important that we use gentle language and loving speech as we talk with people about matters of identity and injustice.

Injustice is suffered by both sides in any personal dispute. It's crucial we understand that. Once understanding and compassion are born in our heart, the poisons of anger, violence, hatred, and despair will be transformed. The path is quite clear. The only solution is to get the poisons out and to get the insight and the compassion in! Then we will discover each other as human beings, not allowing ourselves to be deceived by the outer layers, by names like "Buddhism," "Islam," "Judaism," "pro-American," "pro-Arab," and so on. This is a process of liberation—liberation from our ideas, our ignorance, our tendency to discriminate. The Earth is so beautiful and there is room enough for all of us, yet we kill each other. But when we can see each other as human beings with their own suffering, we won't have the courage to shoot each other. We'll work together for the chance to live peacefully together.

Q. If you're able to reach a state of deep peace and love, are you being helpful to the world?

A. You're helping the world in many ways. The first thing you're doing is being peace, being love; that's already a big contribution. But once you embody peace and love, everything you do will be for peace and love. You won't be able to refrain from doing good things for the world. Like the Buddha, you will be motivated by a very strong desire to go out and help. The person who has become peace and love won't be able to refrain from doing things for the world. And we can always improve. The Buddha was "awake" and he had a Sangha, yet he continued to work and practice. His community was always expanding and while he helped others become teachers, the Buddha continued to practice and teach. If you think your work is finished, it's not. It will never

be. You have to continue. Love is unlimited. Compassion is unlimited. Joy and equanimity are unlimited.

Chapter 5

Sickness and Health, Death and Dying

Q. We've heard about terminally ill people who have prolonged their lives after they started practicing Buddhism and meditation. What is the connection between illness and meditation?

A. The therapeutic power of meditation is very great. The practice of mindful breathing and walking can release the tensions in the body and also in the mind. When the body is allowed to be itself, when we don't work our body too hard, when we don't let the tensions accumulate, then the body's natural capacity to heal itself can begin to work.

Animals are very wise. When a forest animal gets wounded it knows what to do. The wisdom handed down to it by generations of ancestors tells it what to do. The animal finds a quiet place and lies down to rest. It's not interested in food or in running after other animals; it just rests. After several days of lying quietly, the animal is healed, and it gets up and continues on.

We humans have lost the capacity of resting. We

worry too much. We don't allow our bodies to heal. We don't allow our minds to heal. Even when we're given a few weeks of vacation, we don't know how to rest. Our worries, stress, and fear make the situation worse. Meditation can help release the tension, help us embrace our worries, our fear, our anger; and that is very healing. We allow nature to do the work. It's very important to learn again the art of resting and relaxing.

When we're at peace with ourselves, the elements of our body and mind will work together harmoniously, and that is the foundation of health. Different elements of the body will come together and work in harmony. The chemicals in our body will be released in the exact amount we need. We won't overproduce chemicals like adrenaline.

The Buddha speaks about the "second arrow." When an arrow strikes you, you feel pain. If a second arrow comes and strikes you in the same spot, the pain will be ten times worse. The Buddha advised that when you have some pain in your body or your mind, breathe in and out and recognize the significance of that pain but don't exaggerate its importance. If you stop to worry, to be fearful, to protest, to be angry about the pain, then you magnify the pain ten times or more. Your worry is the second arrow. You should protect yourself and not allow the second arrow to come, because the second arrow comes from you.

Q. Is there a spiritual path for those who are fighting incurable diseases?

A. A serious illness can be a kind of mindfulness bell that starts our true practice and gives birth to our spiritual life. So our sickness may contain a positive element which helps us to grow. It's a bell of mindfulness for us and for everyone around us. The practice of acceptance, not worrying about things and enjoying the present moment, has the power of healing for all of us. Many who have had cancer have been able to survive for a long time.

A gentleman from Canada told me when we met for the first time that his doctor had given him two months to live. I said, "Can you enjoy this cup of tea with me? Forget everything else; just become aware that you are still alive and sitting with members of your Sangha. Just focus your attention on the tea and enjoy this moment." And he was able to do it. After having received the Five Mindfulness Trainings and the practice, he went on living for thirteen years. So we never know. Profit from your days, your months, your years, and the teaching and the practice. While you're alive, enjoy every moment and look deeply to touch your true nature of no birth and no death. That cloud in the sky—she cannot die, she can only become snow or rain. To be a cloud floating in the sky is beautiful; but to become rain falling on the ground is also beautiful. With that insight, you'll continue without fear. And if in your daily life you can produce beautiful thoughts, beautiful speech, and compassionate action, you will continue beautifully in the future in many ways. The dissolution of this body is not the end of anything. That insight is crucial for true happiness and non-fear.

Everything can be a bell of mindfulness, including suffering. The suffering of old age, sickness, and death can be a strong bell of mindfulness. They're powerful messengers. So let us be tuned to these bells of mindfulness and move in the direction that humanity should go. Let's take each other's hand and go together, because unless we do it together we have no hope.

Q. Many of us experience chronic depression that is sometimes chemical in origin. Can we heal our depression through the practice or may we also use medications?

A. Our mental formations, our fear, anger, and despair, produce many kinds of chemicals in our bloodstream. The mind influences the body and the body influences the mind. Body and mind inter-are. I'm not against taking medications, but I strongly advocate the practice of mindfulness so that we can rely less and less on these medicines. One day you may find that you're able to do very well without the medicine. We can do a lot to change the way our mind functions. If we're able to change our mental formations, we'll know how to relax, how to embrace and transform our worries and anxieties. And when we change our mental formations, we change the elements of our body, encouraging a healthy balance in the chemicals it produces.

If you feel you still need the medicines, you should take them. But don't rely on them alone; rely on your practice. Environment is very important. For example, genes don't turn on by themselves; the environment turns on our genes. Choose a sane, healthy environment where there are many elements that can water the positive seeds in you, the seeds of joy, compassion, and non-fear. You'll notice that healing takes place quickly. Everything you get in touch with—conversations, films, books, music—should help to turn on the better things in you. When you listen to a Dharma talk, the good seeds in you are watered. When you learn about the compassionate actions of other people, you have more faith in life and in the future, and that waters the seeds of hope and compassion in you. So allow good situations to water the good seeds in you. This is very healing.

We should be able to create healthy environments for our children and for our friends. We can create communities in which we can live more simply and consume much less, so that the members of the community will be happier. If you devote your life to such an activity, building healthy, simple-living communities, you'll get a lot of joy. The people who live with you will know how to smile, how to enjoy every step, how to enjoy the present moment. That helps the process of healing very much.

Q. If we've been suffering with illness for a long time and the pain is great, are we permitted to end our own life, assuming we have discussed this with our family and our Sangha?

A. During the time of the Buddha, there were monks in his community who became very ill. The Buddha gave many discourses on how to practice during the last days of our lives, particularly the Teachings to

Be Given to the Sick and the Five Remembrances.*
We can study them to learn how to help people who
are suffering or dying. We can also learn to apply
these discourses in our own life if we experience a
life-threatening illness. There are ways to lessen our
physical pain. The Buddha helps us to practice feeling less pain in our bodies. We recognize the existence of our physical pain but we don't exaggerate it
through fear or despair.

When you ask whether it's all right to end our lives
if our lives have become unbearable, I say we should
first try to get help. We can't be dogmatic about
euthanasia; we have to examine each case. Sometimes we have to help a person to die, because their
suffering is so intense it would be against the practice
of compassion if we let them continue to suffer. But
it should be done with the collective insight of the
doctors, the families, and the person concerned. The
collective insight of the Sangha, of the community, is
essential in determining what to do in such a case.

If you have a doctor or a friend who knows about
pain, you can ask him or her to tell you that this is
only a physical pain. She can tell you exactly what

---

* See Thich Nhat Hanh, *Chanting from the Heart* (Berkeley, CA: Parallax Press,
2007).

it is, so you will not exaggerate it with strong emotions like fear, anger, or despair. There are also other ways of practicing with pain. You can restore your inner balance so the pain will be bearable. When you water the positive seeds in yourself, you suffer less and feel that you can continue. When you suffer a lot, you may feel you don't have enough strength to be on your own. When a friend comes and holds your hand, you feel as if you can bear your pain and continue. There is strength and happiness within you. When you touch these elements, they will manifest and help restore your balance, and you'll be able to bear your physical pain more easily.

When one of Sister Chan Khong's sisters was dying in hospital, she was in a coma and suffering very much; she was twisting, moaning, and crying all the time. Her husband and children and even the doctors didn't know how to help her. Then Sr. Chan Khong arrived. She was told that her sister couldn't hear her because she was in a coma. So she played her a tape of the monks and nuns of Plum Village chanting the name of Avalokiteshvara in Vietnamese. [*] She put headphones over her sister's ears and turned up the volume. After only half a minute, a miracle hap-

---

[*] Avalokiteshvara is the bodhisattva of great compassion and deep listening.

pened. Her sister became very quiet, and from that moment until she passed away, she no longer cried from her pain.

Sr. Chan Khong's sister had the seed of the practice. She had heard the chanting before and knew it belonged to her spiritual tradition. It became the source of her peace and well-being during the last weeks of her life, when the other people around her hadn't known how to help her get in touch with her seeds of well-being. Those seeds had become weakened, and she'd become overwhelmed by pain and despair. The chanting that penetrated her was able to touch the source of spiritual energy in her. That source of energy gave her enough strength to reestablish the balance she needed.

We have to realize that while we're suffering physical pain, there are still many unpainful elements in us such as solidity, well-being, and trust. For our balance to be restored, we need to touch those seeds. If we're practicing the teachings of the Buddha, we know what to do in that moment for those who are dying or suffering. We know what to do for those who've lost their balance. When the Buddha or his senior disciples visited a dying person, they always knew what to do to help restore their balance so that they would suffer less. The practice is to water the seeds of happiness and well-being in the person; and it always helps.

Q. How can the practice help those who have experienced the death of a loved one through suicide?

A. A person who commits suicide does so because he isn't able to handle his suffering, his pain, and his emotions. If we weren't ready to help before the act, we have to learn from that in order to be ready to help other people who are intending to commit suicide in the future. We still have loved ones living around us, and if we're not attentive one of them may also commit suicide. So if we can learn from the past, then we don't have to suffer anymore, because the loss of one person becomes the condition to help other people. Don't wait until you lose a second loved one in order to learn this. We don't want to allow it to happen again. With that conviction, we practice. It's possible to help a troubled person see that he or she can become a bodhisattva, a great being, helping other people who suffer. This troubled person may not know what to do with his life; we can show him that there's a wonderful way to use his life to help other people suffer less. Many people have done this. If we can help in this way, the one who has gone will be able to smile, because his death will have become very useful.

Q. Our child is gravely ill. How can we transform our fear?

A. If we look deeply into the reality that is inside us and around us, we see that when the conditions are sufficient something can manifest very beautifully, in its entirety. But when conditions aren't sufficient, then part way through that manifestation can be stopped. When we understand that, we don't suffer as much. If this child doesn't continue then he or she will seek other ways in order to come back again.

One year in Plum Village the winter was very warm and the beautiful Japanese quince bloomed earlier than usual in December. While I did walking meditation I said, "Yes, this year we'll have beautiful flowers with which to decorate our Dharma hall on New Year's Day." A week later, a cold snap froze all the buds. While I did walking meditation I said, "No, this year we won't have flowers with which to decorate our Dharma hall." And I thought there would be no more Japanese quince this year, because every bud had been killed. But about ten days later when I was practicing walking meditation I saw new buds coming out again. And I knew that we'd have flowers after all.

When conditions aren't sufficient, the flowers withdraw in order to come forth again. Babies are also like that. If the conditions aren't good for her to continue as a beautiful young person, she'll withdraw in order to come out again in another form at another time. Don't worry. You won't lose her. Allow her to withdraw in order for her to come again. That is true with every species—animals, flowers, fruits, and so on. If parents know how to look with these eyes, then they won't suffer as much. Impermanence is a reality. Wisdom helps us stand firm. We won't collapse, because we know that nothing is lost. When conditions are sufficient, those who we may have thought were lost to us will come out again, as marvelous as before.

Q. Why is there so much obesity in our society? How can I learn to stop overeating?

A. When people can't stop eating, it's because there's a vacuum within them. They're not able to handle their suffering, and the emptiness inside them continues to make them suffer. Going to the kitchen and getting something to eat is a way of forgetting their trouble and malaise. In Plum Village we practice the precept of not eating apart from the community. Each monk and nun has a bowl called the vessel of appropriate measure, so they take only the amount of food they need. You might like to set up a community like that, with joyful people practicing right eating according to the Five Contemplations.[*]

When you're supported by a loving community, you'll be able to cultivate new habits. Mindfulness helps us recognize our habits. We say, "Hello, my habit, I know you are here, pushing me to go to the kitchen and open the refrigerator." When you practice alone, it's difficult. The temptation can be stronger than your mindfulness. When mindfulness is a collective energy, it's much stronger. When you live with three, four, or five members of a community who practice well, then it's easy. Slowly you'll learn new habits. It's wonderful to learn new habits. You can be peaceful and happy during mealtimes. When you eat, you focus your attention on the piece of carrot, the piece of bread that you eat, and you receive it as an ambassador of the cosmos. Every morsel of food is a chance to practice. If you chew your food carefully twenty or thirty times, you'll feel that you

---

[*] The Five Contemplations are listed in Chapter 7.

don't need to eat a lot. Your body will tell you when you should stop. Listen to the body, the body knows.

Q. What will happen to our consciousness after we die?

A. What happens to consciousness when we're still alive? If you can answer that question, the other question will be answered as well.

We should train ourselves to have eyes that can recognize reality without the forms that we're used to perceiving. When you look at a young cornstalk, you no longer see the seed of corn that's given life to the plant. But looking deeply you can still see the seed of corn in her new form: the cornstalk. This is a deep practice. It's a door of liberation from fear, craving, and despair.

We haven't been able to see ourselves clearly and deeply. We're not able to see other people clearly and deeply. We're very much on the surface of things. We don't know who we really are, or who they really are. That's why our notions of birth and death, of being and non-being are also very shallow. The practice of Buddhist meditation is to get deeper into your perception of what is there. When you look at a person, like your beloved, look deeply. Don't wait until that person dies in order to look for him or for her. Look right now. Looking deeply we see cells in the body operating together, flowing like a river. We see a river of feelings, many feelings succeeding each other. We see a river of perception. We see a river of mental formations, and we see a river of consciousness. Consciousness isn't an unchanging permanent entity; it's a process, a stream. Looking deeply we see that our body is also not a solid thing but a process. The birth and the death of all the cells is continuous; they succeed each other.

Looking deeply with the eyes of signlessness, will help you to transcend a person's outer form. If you're capable of seeing him or her with the eyes of signlessness, you won't grieve when that appearance is no longer there. Because even when that appearance is gone, your beloved is still somewhere. The disintegration of this body is nothing at all. Nothing is lost. If we don't have this form, we have another form. If we don't have the cloud, we have the rain. If we don't have the rain, we have the tea. That is the practice. Your body, your presence, and your consciousness overlap and occupy all of time and space. In that sense there is no "before" and "after" we die. We should generate enough of the energy of mindfulness and concentration so we're able to have this awareness. Then we'll transcend the notion of birth and death.

Q. What can help us take comfort that our loved ones will continue on in other forms after they die?

A. When you look at an orange tree, you see that the orange tree is producing beautiful green leaves, fragrant orange blossoms, and sweet oranges. Those are the things an orange tree has to offer to the world. A human being is like that too. In her daily life she produces thoughts, speech, and actions. Our thoughts may be beautiful, compassionate, and loving. Our speech may also be compassionate, inspiring, full of love and understanding. And our actions may also be compassionate, protecting, healing, and supporting others and ourselves. Looking deeply in the present moment we can see that we're producing thoughts, speech, and actions. In the Buddhist tradition, our thoughts, our speech and our actions are our true continuation.

Once we've produced a thought it will be here for a long time. Once we've said something, our words will remain for a long time. Once we've taken an action, our action can have an effect far into the future. Suppose you produce a thought of compassion and forgiveness. Right away that thought has a healing effect on your body and your mind. It also has an immediate healing effect on the world, and it will continue to have a healing effect into the future. So it's very important to be able to produce a thought of compassion, nondiscrimination, and forgiveness.

Many people believe that after the disintegration of the body there's nothing left. Even many scientists still believe that. But our thoughts, our speech, and our actions are the energies we produce, and they will continue for a long time. We can assure a beautiful continuation by producing good thoughts, speech, and action. You can't destroy a human being. You can't reduce him or her to nonbeing. Just as it's impossible for a cloud to die, it's impossible for a human being to become nothing. So looking deeply like that into our true nature, looking deeply into the nature of other people around you, you'll have the kind of insight that will liberate you from sorrow, fear, and anger. Non-fear, the insight that there's no birth and no death, is the greatest gift given to us by the practice of looking deeply.

Chapter 6

Children's Questions

Q. Who was the Buddha?

A. The Buddha was a person, just like you and me. He was a prince named Siddhartha, who lived in Nepal about 2,600 years ago. He had everything he could want: a beautiful palace, wealth, the best foods, luxurious vacations, and plenty of power. He was a very good student. He learned very well. He grew up, got married, and had a little boy. But he wasn't happy. He knew something important was missing in his life. Although his father tried to hide all human suffering from him, Siddhartha saw how much people were suffering, and he saw how little his father, the king, was able to do to help them.

His father wanted him to become king, but Siddhartha didn't want to be king. Instead, he determined to become a monk, in order to liberate himself from suffering so that he could help others. Siddhartha left the royal palace during the night, leaving behind his wife and his son, and he went to the woods and practiced as a monk for many years. Finally he became a buddha, a fully enlightened person. Then he began to teach. He taught for forty-five years and helped many people—rich people, poor people, all kinds of people, and he had many students. He died at the age of eighty. His teaching has been handed down through the generations, and now we are his students.

The Buddha said that every one of us can become a buddha like him. If we have love, understanding, and peace, if we can transform our anger, our jealousy, then we can become a buddha like him. And in the cosmos there are many other buddhas. Wherever there are human beings, there is the possibility of a buddha, or many buddhas, manifesting.

Q. What does "Dharma" mean?

A. The Dharma is the practice of love and understanding. The Dharma may be in the form of a Dharma talk, or perhaps in the form of a book. The best Dharma is the living Dharma embodied by a practitioner. When you look at that practitioner you see the presence of peace, loving kindness, understanding, and compassion. That is the living Dharma. When you practice mindful breathing, calming your mind, calming your feelings, that is the living Dharma.

The Buddha passed on the Dharma to many generations. Now you and I are the continuation of the Buddha and thanks to our practice, we keep the Dharma alive so that we can pass it on. The Dharma is the essence of a Buddha. With the Dharma, people suffer less and they can be happy and loving. Without the Dharma inside, the Buddha is not a Buddha. Without the Dharma inside, a Sangha is not a true Sangha. Your practice is to keep the Dharma alive and growing every day, for your own happiness and for the happiness of other people. When you embody the Dharma in that way, we call it the "Dharma body."

Q. What is the most important thing we can do to become enlightened?

A. Enlightenment isn't something that's far away. You don't need to practice for a long time to get enlightened. You can be enlightened right here and right now to some degree. It's like health and wellbeing. When you drink your tea and you know that you're drinking your tea, you're concentrated, you see that drinking tea is something you like to do. So drinking tea mindfully is a kind of enlightenment. There are many people who drink their tea but who don't know that they're drinking their tea. They're so absorbed in their anger, their fear, their worries, and their projects that they don't even notice the tea. Being mindful of what's happening in the present moment is enlightenment. When you walk like a sleepwalker, there's no enlightenment. When you walk mindfully and enjoy every step you make, enlightenment is already there. When you eat mindfully, there is enlightenment. We call it mindfulness, but mindfulness is the beginning of enlightenment. If we continue to live mindfully every moment of our daily life, our mindfulness will grow strong and powerful. That's why we have the saying, "There's no way to enlightenment, enlightenment is the way." Enlightenment must be in the here and the now. You drink your tea, you walk, you breathe, you sit, you wash your clothes in such a way that happiness is possible right now and right here. That is our practice.

Q. What is the best way to meditate?

A. We can meditate in the sitting position, but we can also meditate while we're walking or standing. Meditation can be very informal. Suppose you're standing in line, waiting your turn to serve yourself some food. You might practice mindful breathing in and out, enjoying yourself and the presence of the people around you. When you ride your bicycle, if you ride mindfully, enjoying your in-breath and out-breath, you're practicing meditation. When you wash the dishes, if you enjoy breathing in and breathing out and if you smile, the dishwashing becomes very pleasant. So meditation is possible in all kinds of positions, whether lying down, standing, walking, sitting, or doing things. Everything you do, if you do it mindfully, is meditation.

Q. How do we overcome fear?

A. First you must find out whether your fear has been born from your wrong perception. The practice of mindful breathing in and out, deep and slow, can help you to look deeply into the nature and roots of your fear. People are afraid of dying, people are afraid of getting old, of being abandoned. People are afraid of being sick. People are afraid of losing what they cherish today, of losing the people they love today, of losing their jobs and so on. The Buddha advises us not to try to run away from our fear, but to bring up our fear and have a deep look into it. Most of us try to cover up our fear. Most of us are afraid of looking directly at our fear. Instead of trying to distract yourself from this fear, or ignore it, the Buddha proposed that you bring the seed of fear up and recognize that it's there and embrace it with your mindfulness. Sitting with your fear, instead of trying to push it away or bury it, can transform it. This is true of all of your fears, both small ones and big ones. You don't have to try and convince yourself not to be afraid. You don't have to try and fight or overcome your fear. Over time you'll find that when your fear comes up again, it will be a little bit weaker.

Q. How can we deal with anger?

A. Sometimes we're angry, but we don't accept that we're angry. In that case we need a friend who's honest enough to say, "Dear friend, you're angry." But if you're a good practitioner you don't need a friend to tell you, because you practice mindfulness and you're aware of what's happening inside you. When anger comes up, you know it's there. So you practice mindful breathing and say,

Breathing in, I know anger is in me.
Breathing out, I take good care of my anger.

Don't say or do anything else because saying or doing something in anger can be very destructive. Just go home to yourself and continue to practice mindful breathing and mindful walking to embrace, recognize, and bring relief to your anger. After that look deeply into your anger and ask yourself what has caused it.

We may be the main cause of our own suffering and anger because often the seed of anger in us is already too big. As soon as we hear or see something unpleasant, that seed in us is watered and we become angry. So, our suffering comes mostly from us, and not from another person. The other person is just a secondary cause. Look deeply into your anger, and you might see that your anger has been created by your wrong perceptions, wrong views, and misunderstanding; and when you realize that, your anger is transformed.

Q. I worry so much that it's hard for me to do whatever I need to do. How can I stop worrying?

A. The practice is to learn to take care of the present moment. Don't allow yourself to be lost in the past or the future. Taking good care of the present moment, we may be able to change the negative things in the past and prepare for a good future. We tend to worry about what will happen in the future. The practice helps us to come home to the present moment, to our body, our feelings, to the environment around us. When we breathe in and breathe out mindfully, our mind is brought back to our body and we are truly there in order to take care of the present moment. If there's some stress, some tension in our body, we practice mindful breathing in order to release the tension, and that brings us relief. If there's a painful feeling in us, we use mindfulness to embrace our feeling so that we can get relief. The key point is that you are fully there in the present moment, in the here and the now, to take care of yourself and what's happening around you. You don't think too much about the future or project too much about how it might be; and you're not trapped too much in the past. You have to train yourself, to learn how to go home to the present moment, to the here and the now, and to take care of that moment, to take care of your body and your feelings in this moment. That is the most effective way to deal with anxiety or worries.

As you learn how to handle the present moment, you'll gain faith and trust in your ability to handle the situation. You learn how to take care of your feelings and what's happening around you. That makes you confident; and as your confidence grows, you're no longer the victim of your worries.

Q. When someone dies, does their knowledge go to waste?

A. In the teaching of the Buddha, nothing can disappear. When your body disintegrates, that's not your end. This body is only a very small part of you. We human beings produce speech, thinking, and bodily actions. That is our continuation. In Buddhism we call it karma. Karma means action: action in thought, speech, and deed. As soon as we produce a thought, that thought will have an impact right away on us and on the world. That thought is our continuation. And you *are* that thought. A thought of compassion, forgiveness, and understanding will have a good effect on your body, your mind, and on the world. A thought of anger, hatred, or violence will have a negative effect on your body, your mind, and on the world; and that's not such a beautiful continuation. Your practice is to keep producing beautiful thoughts—thoughts of compassion, understanding, and forgiveness. The Buddha describes that as the practice of "right thinking."

153

What you produce every day as thought, speech, and action is out in the world, even though you don't see it. It's like water vapor in the air—we can't see but we know it's there. Your thoughts, speech, and actions are your continuation. So when you look at your body, you have to learn to see that this is only a small part of you. It's like a rain cloud up in the sky that looks down and sees that half of herself is already down on Earth in the form of a river. The cloud in the sky smiles to the cloud on Earth and says, "Enjoy your journey, I will join you soon." You can be that cloud looking at the part of yourself that's already in the future and say, "Enjoy your journey, I will join you soon." Your intelligence, your love, your hate, your joy, your peace, your suffering are not only here, but are also there, as your continuation.

Q. What should I do when other children tease me?

A. When other children tease us, we may get angry, we may say something unkind, or we may do something to punish them, and that isn't good. As a practitioner, you go back to your in-breath and your out-breath and you keep your cool and you say to yourself, "This is a challenge. If I can stay calm I'm a good practitioner. If I react violently, I'll suffer, and that's not being a good practitioner." So go back to your in-breath, your out-breath, breathe in peacefully and breathe out peacefully, and smile at the child who's teasing you. When you can look at that child with compassion you feel much better. You're acting like a young Buddha, responding to provocation with a smile, with loving kindness and compassion. That will disarm the person who is teasing you. If you can do that, it's a big victory!

Q. How can I control my temper?

A. The better way is not to control, but to be with it, to make friends with it. As soon as you try to control, there may be a battle going on between you and your temper. So it's better not to control, but to be with it and to take care of it. It's the same when you're angry or fearful—you don't fight your anger or fear, you just recognize that you're angry or afraid.

Breathing in, I know I am angry.
Breathing out, I embrace and recognize my anger.
I know I am taking good care of my anger.

The best way to deal with our temper is to be with it and take care of it, like a big brother taking care of his young brother or sister. It's better not to fight. In the Buddhist tradition of meditation, there's no fighting, just recognizing, embracing, and helping.

Q. I go to a Catholic school, and some of my friends say Catholicism is the only true religion. How can I show them that being Catholic is not the only way to spiritual fulfillment?

A. There are many spiritual traditions in the world. One tradition doesn't have to exclude the others. Each tradition belongs to the spiritual heritage of humankind. We have to cherish all of them. It's like a bowl of fruit. If you love oranges, you have the freedom to eat oranges; but nobody forbids you to enjoy apples, peaches, and plums as well. It would be very sad if you ate only oranges. Many of us enjoy the teachings and the practice of Buddhism, but we also enjoy the teachings and the practice of Islam, Christianity, Judaism, and so on. We can learn from other traditions. Those who say that theirs is the only tradition are like people who eat only one kind of fruit. They have no capacity to enjoy other traditions, other fruits. They're missing out on so much.

We feel sorry for them. We try to help them to see that they can enjoy more if they have the attitude of openness. Slowly, patiently, with loving kindness, you can help people to open up.

Q. Can we remember any of our past lives?

A. When I practice looking deeply into myself I see that in the past I have been a rock, a tree, a squirrel, a bird, a fish, a cloud, a river. And if I look deeply I see that I am still a rock, a tree, a squirrel, a bird, a fish, a cloud, a river—I continue to be these things. You think you're only a human being, but if you look deeply, you see that you are, at the same time, many other things. Think about it. You may believe the clouds are up there in the sky, but the clouds are truly in you. When you drink a cup of tea mindfully, deeply, in meditation, you see that you are drinking a cloud. Drinking a cloud is what we do every day, but we don't realize it. The cloud has become rain, the rain has become tea, and you are drinking the cloud in the form of tea. With the practice of look-ing deeply we can see our former lives, and we see how we continue to carry our former lives with us in the present moment. Past lives are not imagination. We have evolved from rock to water to single-celled beings to human beings. We have all gone through many states of being, and we continue to be these things; we inter-are with them.

Q. What will happen to the other monks and nuns, and to the Sangha, when you're gone?

A. I will always be here. I have tried my best to transmit myself to everyone. I am not outside of you, I am inside of you. And a true Sangha, a Sangha that practices well, always has the Buddha, the Dharma, and her teacher inside of her. So wherever you are, if you feel that the Sangha, the Buddha, the Dharma are within you, there is no separation. As we continue to practice, we realize that they are all in our heart. It takes a little bit of time and practice to realize that truth. When we bow to the Buddha, we may think that the Buddha is seated on the altar. But the Buddha isn't on the altar; the Buddha is in our hearts. Because the Buddha is the capacity to be mindful, to be awakened, to be loving, to be accepting, and we know that in our hearts there are such capacities too. If we practice well, these capacities will develop. So the idea of outside and inside will become clearer. We have to look deeply to see that the one we love and respect is really within ourselves.

Q. What should I do when I feel sad?

A. It's okay to feel sad. It's good not to rush away from your sadness and to just let yourself be sad for a little while. But you can also change the situation with the practice. When you're sad, there are many things that can cheer you up. I have a special meditation called pebble meditation that you can use to cheer up yourself or your friends.*

Mindful breathing can also transform your sadness. With our breath, we can bring peace to our breath, to our body, and to our feelings. With the power of our mindful in-breath and out-breath we can help calm our body and our feelings and our mind. With still water there is no fighting. The time when we are sad is a good time to cultivate the quality of stillness and peace in us.

Q. Why do kids watch television?

A. Because their parents are too busy. The television becomes a babysitter. Watching television sometimes can be very good, because there are good programs on television. You can learn a lot by watching

---

* Pebble meditation is detailed in Chapter 7.

these programs that can teach us and show us many interesting things. But there are also violent programs and others that try and convince you that to be happy you need to have your parents buy you many things. That's why it's not good for children to watch a lot of TV. If grownups were not so busy, they could spend more time with their children, and children wouldn't have to watch as much. There are many wonderful things to do that can bring us a lot of joy, so that we don't need to watch television anymore. Once we had a retreat where 300 children came. In the beginning, many of them protested because there was no television and there were no electronic games. But they all had so much fun at the retreat they forgot all about television. And they survived very well! That's why we have to think of all the other wonderful things that can replace television.

Q. Are Buddhists allowed to go fishing?

A. According to the Two Promises, we must try to protect the lives of people, animals, plants, and minerals.

I vow to develop understanding in order to live peacefully with people, animals, plants, and minerals.

I vow to develop my compassion, in order to protect the lives of people, animals, plants, and minerals.

So going fishing would break your promise. Suppose you're a daughter fish or a son fish. You're having a good time swimming, and suddenly you're caught by a fisherman. You can never go back to your father fish and your mother fish. I think they will suffer. That's why refraining from fishing is practicing compassion. Allow them to have a chance to live.

But every living being has to live and has to get food. That's why we have to go fishing from time to time, otherwise we'd starve. The principle is that when you don't need to fish, when you don't need to kill an animal for food, you don't do it. That's how the animals practice also. A lion hunts only when she, her mate, and her cubs are hungry. When lions aren't hungry, they don't hunt. Humans have to learn from animals. Animals don't destroy or kill unless they need food to eat. And the practice, the promise, is to bring happiness and joy to ourselves and happiness and joy to other living beings. We try to do our best. No one can practice the non-killing precept in a perfect way.

Even the Buddha can't practice the First Promise perfectly, because he has to walk and he has to eat.

When he walks, he might crush little creatures under his feet, even if he doesn't mean to. During the time of the Buddha, attending the three months retreat was prescribed for monks during the rainy season so they could avoid traveling during that time and stepping on the many living beings that come out with the rains. When we walk on the grass we may kill little living beings in the grass. There's a very moving poem about this in a book I wrote for for new monks and nuns.* You can practice this verse while breathing in and out, when you wake up in the morning and your feet are looking for your slippers, or when you're putting on your shoes to get ready for school:

From early morning until late in the evening
Every living being has to take care of his or her life.
Little insect, if by chance I step on you and kill you
May you be reborn right away in the Pure Land of the Buddha.

Even when we eat a vegetarian meal we still have to boil our vegetables, and when we boil vegetables we may boil small creatures like insects and bacteria. So

---

* Thich Nhat Hanh, *Stepping into Freedom* (Berkeley, CA: Parallax Press, 1997).

a vegetarian dish is never absolutely vegetarian.

The idea is that we try our best to protect life, knowing that we cannot be perfect. If we're doing our best, that's good enough. You don't have to be perfect in compassion. But if you know that every day you make a little progress on the path of compassion, you have peace and you contribute peace to the world. Going in the direction of reverence for life is good, because going in that direction you're saving human life, saving the life of animals, plants, and minerals.

Q. Jesus and Martin Luther King, Jr. and Gandhi were killed and you were exiled from Vietnam. Why do bad things happen to spiritual people?

A. When people are full of misunderstanding and fear, they can do violent things. They thought of Martin Luther King, Jr. as a dangerous person, Mahatma Gandhi as a dangerous person, Jesus as a dangerous person. That's wrong perception. And wrong perception is the ground of all kinds of fear and anger. So our practice should be helping to remove wrong perceptions. Spiritual leaders like Gandhi and Dr. King were not angry when they died. They felt compassion even toward the people who killed them, because they knew it was wrong perception, anger, and fear that led someone to commit that kind of action. Our world needs a lot of compassion and understanding, and our practice should be able to bring about more understanding and compassion.

Looking deeply we remove our wrong views, and from there understanding and compassion will arise. Practicing the Dharma, using loving speech and deep listening, we can help each other remove wrong perceptions so that people will no longer be fearful and angry. That's what we should do in order to stop wars, prevent terrorism, wipe out violence, and make peace. You can't prevent terrorism with bombs and guns. Using bombs and guns only produces more terrorists and makes terrorism stronger. Each of us has seeds of understanding and compassion. That's what we call the Buddha nature. The practice is to touch the seeds in us that are wholesome and help them to grow every day.

Q. How can we help others to let go of their fear of physical pain and death?

A. First we have to help ourselves. We should know how to handle our own fear and pain. After that, we can help other people because we have direct experience about how to handle the fear and the pain. Suffering and fear are not things that just we experience by ourselves. Our fear and suffering is also the suffering of our parents and our friends. You are me and I am you. If something wonderful happens to one of us, it happens to all of us. If something awful happens to one of us, it happens to all of us. So in that light, the child is the adult and the adult is the child. This answer comes from the insight of no-self. With the insight of no-self you see that your suffering, your fear, is a collective suffering. With the insight of no-self, you see that happiness is collective happiness. We're not separated.

Suppose you practice to release the tension, the stress, the pain in your body, and then you feel better. You know how to practice like this very well. Now when you see a person who is tense, who has pain in his or her body, you can show him or her how to practice. That person will believe you because you have direct experience. You've walked your talk. That's why it's very important that we're able to do it for ourselves first. Just the way you live your life, the way you react to situations, can already be very helpful. Other people see you react in a peaceful and kind way, and they already begin to learn from you.

Q. What does the mindfulness bell mean?

A. The mindfulness bell helps us to go home to ourselves, to enjoy our mindful breathing, and to realize that we are alive, we are here, sitting and walking on this beautiful planet. The bell is like a friend calling you back to the present moment. Many kinds of sounds can be mindfulness bells. The temple bell, the church bell, we even consider the sound of a phone to be a kind of mindfulness bell.

Telephone meditation is wonderful. First of all you pick up a phone (it can be a cell phone or traditional telephone) and practice breathing in and out to calm yourself. Then you say:

Words can travel thousands of miles.
Words can help restore communication and build up mutual understanding.
I vow that the conversation I'm going to have will bring us closer together,
And make our friendship bloom like a flower.

You breathe in and breathe out, as you recite these verses and then you dial the number. The telephone on the other end begins to ring, and because that person is also practicing telephone meditation and practicing breathing in and out when she hears the telephone, you know that she will not answer before three rings. She's saying:

I listen, I listen.
The mindfulness bell of the telephone
brings me back to my true home.

So you continue to breathe in and out, enjoying your in-breath and your out-breath while you wait for her to answer the phone. When she picks up the telephone, the conversation must be good, must be joyful, because both of you are practicing and are calm and smiling. That's what we call telephone meditation. I have many friends, including executives, who enjoy telephone meditation. They report that they enjoy doing business more when they practice that way.

In Plum Village every time the phone rings everyone practices mindful breathing in and out. So the bell is a friend, an invention of practitioners to help us. If you work on a computer you might get so carried away by your work that you forget that you're alive. So you may like to program your computer so that every quarter of an hour it offers the sound of the bell enabling you to go back to yourself, to smile and breathe in and out before you continue work. Many of our friends have done that. A bell reminding you to come back to yourself and enjoy breathing is a wonderful way to take a break.

Chapter 7

Practices for Daily Mindfulness

THE FIVE MINDFULNESS TRAININGS

The First Mindfulness Training
Aware of the suffering caused by the destruction of life, I am committed to cultivating compassion and learning ways to protect the lives of people, animals, plants, and minerals. I am determined not to kill, not to let others kill, and not to support any act of killing in the world, in my thinking, and in my way of life.

The Second Mindfulness Training
Aware of the suffering caused by exploitation, social injustice, stealing, and oppression, I am committed to cultivating loving kindness and learning ways to work for the well-being of people, animals, plants, and minerals. I will practice generosity by sharing my time, energy, and material resources with those who are in real need. I am determined not to steal and not to possess anything that should belong to others. I will respect the property of others, but I

will prevent others from profiting from human suffering or the suffering of other species on Earth.

The Third Mindfulness Training

Aware of the suffering caused by sexual misconduct, I am committed to cultivating responsibility and learning ways to protect the safety and integrity of individuals, couples, families, and society. I am determined not to engage in sexual relations without love and a long-term commitment. To preserve the happiness of myself and others, I am determined to respect my commitments and the commitments of others. I will do everything in my power to protect children from sexual abuse and to prevent couples and families from being broken by sexual misconduct.

The Fourth Mindfulness Training

Aware of the suffering caused by unmindful speech and the inability to listen to others, I am committed to cultivating loving speech and deep listening in order to bring joy and happiness to others and relieve others of their suffering. Knowing that words can create happiness or suffering, I am determined to speak truthfully, with words that inspire self-confidence, joy, and hope. I will not spread news that I do not know to be certain and will not criticize or condemn things of which I am not sure. I will refrain from uttering words that can cause division or discord, or that can cause the family or the community to break. I am determined to make all efforts to reconcile and resolve all conflicts, however small.

The Fifth Mindfulness Training

Aware of the suffering caused by unmindful consumption, I am committed to cultivating good health, both physical and mental, for myself, my family, and my society by practicing mindful eating, drinking, and consuming. I will ingest only items that preserve peace, well-being, and joy in my body, in my consciousness, and in the collective body and consciousness of my family and society. I am determined not to use alcohol or any other intoxicant or to ingest foods or other items that contain toxins, such as certain TV programs, magazines, books, films, and conversations. I am aware that to damage my body or my consciousness with these poisons is to betray my ancestors, my parents, my society, and future generations. I will work to transform violence, fear, anger, and confusion in myself and in society by practicing a diet for myself and for society. I understand that a proper diet is crucial for self-transformation and for the transformation of society.

THE FIVE CONTEMPLATIONS

This food is a gift of the earth, the sky, numerous living beings, and much hard work.

May we eat with mindfulness and gratitude so as to be worthy to receive it.

May we recognize and transform our unwholesome mental formations, especially our greed, and learn to eat with moderation.

May we keep our compassion alive by eating in such a way that we reduce the suffering of living beings, preserve our planet and reverse the process of global warming.

We accept this food so that we may nurture our sisterhood and brotherhood, strengthen our Sangha and nourish our ideal of serving all beings.

THE FIVE REMEMBRANCES

*These Five Remembrances help us to identify and look deeply at
the seeds of fear. They can be recited daily, read aloud as a guided
meditation, or used as a silent meditation by individual practitioners.*

I am of the nature to grow old.
There is no way to escape growing old.

I am of the nature to have ill-health.
There is no way to escape having ill-health.

I am of the nature to die.
There is no way to escape death.

All that is dear to me and everyone I love are of the nature to change.
There is no way to escape being separated from them.

I inherit the results of my actions of body, speech, and mind.
My actions are my continuation.

MINDFUL WALKING

The mind can go in a thousand directions.
But on this beautiful path, I walk in peace.
With each step, a gentle wind blows.
With each step, a flower blooms.

Walking meditation is meditation while walking. We walk slowly, in a relaxed way, keeping a light smile on our lips. When we practice this way, we feel deeply at ease, and our steps are those of the most secure person on Earth. Walking meditation is really to enjoy the walking—walking not in order to arrive, but just for walking, to be in the present moment, and to enjoy each step. Therefore you have to shake off all worries and anxieties, not thinking of the future, not thinking of the past, just enjoying the present moment. Anyone can do it. It takes only a little time, a little mindfulness, and the wish to be happy.

We walk all the time, but usually it is more like running. Our hurried steps print anxiety and sorrow on the Earth. If we can take one step in peace, we can take two, three, four, and then five steps for the peace and happiness of humankind.

Our mind darts from one thing to another, like a monkey swinging from branch to branch without stopping to rest. Thoughts have millions of pathways, and we are forever pulled along by them into the world of forgetfulness. If we can transform our walking path into a field for meditation, our feet will take every step in full awareness, our breathing will be in harmony with our steps, and our mind will naturally be at ease. Every step we take will reinforce our peace and joy and cause a stream of calm energy to flow through us. Then we can say, "With each step, a gentle wind blows."

While walking, practice conscious breathing by counting steps. Notice each breath and the number of steps you take as you breathe in and as you breathe out. If you take three steps during an in-breath, say, silently, "One, two, three," or "In, in, in," one word with each step. As you breathe out, if you take three steps, say, "Out, out, out," with each step. If you take three steps as you breathe in and four steps as you breathe out, you say, "In, in, in. Out, out, out, out," or "One, two, three. One, two, three, four."

Don't try to control your breathing. Allow your lungs as much time and air as they need, and simply notice how many steps you take as your lungs fill up and how many you take as they empty, mindful of both your breath and your steps. The key is mindfulness.

When you walk uphill or downhill, the number of steps per breath will change. Always follow the needs of your lungs. Do not try to control your breathing or your walking. Just observe them deeply.

When you begin to practice, your exhalation may be longer than your inhalation. You might find that you take three steps during your in-breath and four steps on your out-breath (3-4), or two steps/three steps (2-3). If this is comfortable for you, please enjoy practicing this way. After you have been doing walking meditation for some time, your in-breath and out-breath will probably become equal: 3-3, or 2-2, or 4-4.

If you see something along the way that you want to touch with your mindfulness—the blue sky, the hills, a tree, or a bird—just stop, but while you do, continue breathing mindfully. You can keep the object of your contemplation alive by means of mindful breathing. If you don't breathe consciously, sooner or later your thinking will settle back in, and the bird or the tree will disappear. Always stay with your breathing.

When you walk, you might like to take the hand of a child. She will receive your concentration and stability, and you will receive her freshness and innocence. From time to time, she may want to run ahead and then wait for you to catch up. A child is a bell of mindfulness, reminding us how wonderful life is. At Plum Village, I teach the young people a simple verse to practice while walking: "Yes, yes, yes," as they breathe in, and, "Thanks, thanks, thanks," as they breathe out. I want them to respond to life, to society, and to the Earth in a positive way. They enjoy it very much.

After you have been practicing for a few days, try adding one more step to your exhalation. For example, if your normal breathing is 2-2, without walking any faster, lengthen your exhalation and practice 2-3 for four or five times. Then go back to 2-2. In normal breathing, we never expel all the air from our lungs. There is always some left. By adding another step to your exhalation, you will push out more of this stale air. Don't overdo it. Four or five times are enough. More can make you tired. After breathing this way four or five times, let your breath return to normal. Then, five or ten minutes later, you can repeat the process. Remember to add a step to the exhalation, not the inhalation.

After practicing for a few more days, your lungs might say to you, "If we could do 3-3 instead of 2-3, that would be wonderful." If the message is clear, try it, but even then, only do it four or five times. Then go back to 2-2. In five or ten minutes, begin 2-3, and then do 3-3 again. After several months, your lungs will be healthier and your blood will circulate better. Your way of breathing will have been transformed.

When we practice walking meditation, we arrive in each moment. When we enter the present moment deeply, our regrets and sorrows disappear, and we discover life with all its wonders. Breathing in, we say to ourselves, "I have arrived." Breathing out, we say, "I am home." When we do this, we overcome dispersion and dwell peacefully in the present moment, which is the only moment for us to be alive.

You can also practice walking meditation using the lines of a poem. In Zen Buddhism, poetry and practice always go together.

I have arrived.
> *I am home*
> *in the here,*
> *in the now.*
> *I am solid.*
> *I am free.*
> *In the ultimate*
> *I dwell.*

As you walk, be fully aware of your foot, the ground, and the connection between them, which is your conscious breathing. People say that walking on water is a miracle, but to me, walking peacefully on the Earth is the real miracle. The Earth is a miracle. Each step is a miracle. Taking steps on our beautiful planet can bring real happiness.

PEBBLE MEDITATION

Although this meditation is usually introduced to children, it is a very useful practice for adults as well.

First of all, collect four pebbles from outside and wash them. If you like, you can make a little cloth bag to put them in. Then sit down with your pebbles. If someone has a bell, they can invite the bell while you enjoy breathing in and breathing out. Then take the pebbles out of the bag and put them on your left. With your right hand pick up the first pebble and look at it.

After looking at the first pebble and recognizing that it's representing a flower, you put it on the palm of your left hand and you put one hand over the other and you begin your meditation on flowerness. You can say three times: "Breathing in, I see myself as a flower. Breathing out, I feel fresh." You are really a flower in the garden of humanity. This exercise will restore your freshness, your flowerness. It's very helpful to smile during the practice, because a flower is always smiling. Your in-breath and out-breath help you to become a flower again. Then put the pebble down on your right.

Then pick up the second pebble and look at it. This one represents a mountain, solidity. When you're solid and stable you are yourself. Without solidity, you can't truly be happy. When we're not solidly established in the present moment, we can be pulled away by people provoking us, by our anger, fear, regret, or anxiety. Restoring our solidity is very important. This meditation is best practiced in the sitting position so your body feels very stable and solid. Even if someone were to come and push you, you wouldn't fall over. After you've put the second pebble in your left hand, you begin to meditate on the mountain. You can say three times: *"Breathing in, I see myself as a mountain. Breathing out, I feel solid."*

The third pebble represents still water. Sometimes you see a lake where the water is so still that it reflects exactly what is there: the blue sky, the white clouds, the mountains, the trees—it's so still. When our mind is calm it is like that lake; it reflects things as they are, and we're not victims of wrong perception. When our mind is disturbed by craving, anger, jealousy, then we're no longer lucid, calm, and serene, and we perceive things in the wrong way. Wrong perceptions bring us a lot of anger and fear, and push us to do and say things that destroy everything. That's why we have to practice to restore our calm and our peace that are represented by the still water. You can say three times: *"Breathing in, I see myself as still water.*

Breathing out, I reflect things as they truly are."

The fourth pebble represents space and freedom. If you don't have enough space in your heart, it's very difficult for you to feel happy. If you've ever arranged flowers, you know that each flower needs space around her in order to radiate her beauty. For that reason you don't need a lot of flowers, only a few. Each of us is a flower. Each of us needs some space around us and inside us. If you love someone, one of the most precious things you can offer them is space. This is something you can't buy in the supermarket. Use your imagination and visualize the moon sailing in the sky; she has a lot of space around her, and that is why the moon is so beautiful. The Buddha has been described by many of his disciples as the full moon sailing in the empty sky. You can say three times: *"Breathing in, I see myself as space. Breathing out, I feel free."*

If I don't have any pebbles with me, I sometimes just sing this song:

Flower, fresh.

Mountain, solid.

Water, reflecting.

Space, free.

**PARALLAX
PRESS**

Parallax Press is a nonprofit publisher, founded and inspired by Zen Master Thich Nhat Hanh. We publish books on mindfulness in daily life and are committed to making these teachings accessible to everyone and preserving them for future generations. We do this work to alleviate suffering and contribute to a more just and joyful world. For a copy of the catalog, please contact:

Parallax Press
P.O. Box 7355
Berkeley, CA 94707
www.parallax.org

Monastics and laypeople practice the art of mindful living in the tradition of Thich Nhat Hanh at retreat communities worldwide. To reach any of these communities, or for information about individuals and families joining for a practice period, please contact:

Plum Village
13 Martineau
33580 Dieulivol, France
www.plumvillage.org

Blue Cliff Monastery
3 Mindfulness Road
Pine Bush, NY 12566
www.bluecliffmonastery.org

Blue Cliff Monastery
123 Towles Rd.
Batesville, MS 38606
magnoliagrovemonastery.org

Deer Park Monastery
2499 Melru Lane
Escondido, CA 92026
www.deerparkmonastery.org

The Mindfulness Bell, a journal of the art of mindful living in the tradition of Thich Nhat Hanh, is published three times a year by Plum Village. To subscribe or to see the worldwide directory of Sanghas, visit **mindfulnessbell.org**.